Library of Congress Control Number:    2009910419
ISBN:          Hardcover          978-1-4415-8700-8
               Softcover          978-1-4415-8699-5

First Edition 2009

This book was printed in the United States of America by Xlibris Corporation
1 888 795 4274
www.Xlibris.com

Author and front cover photographs by Rav Holly - www.ravholly.com

**To order additional copies of this book, go to:**
www.stopblamingthesoftware.com

# Stop Blaming the Software

Corporate Profiling for Project Success

## Acknowledgments

This book is for you Mark, my husband and friend. Thank you for your constant support, encouragement, and patience.

*"A man can fail many times, but he isn't a failure until he begins to blame somebody else"*

Author and Naturalist John Burroughs (1837-1921).

# CONTENTS

# PREFACE

Stephen Manes, commenting on the changes he has observed over the past 25 years. Full Disclosure, Stephen Manes, PCWorld, December 2008.

# Preface

Why do we expect IT projects to go according to plan, while we simultaneously harbor expectations of failure? This is a paradox we mentally juggle, albeit only fleetingly, when we start an IT project. If we have communicated widely, decided collaboratively, and planned extensively, then why do our concerns and nagging doubts persist as the project progresses? With the absence of any rational answers to our concerns, and with failed IT projects typically dominated by biased opinions, scapegoats, finger pointing and refutations, there has been a crucial need for research to uncover the root causes of failed IT projects.

My approach to the research behind this book comes from the perspective of pre-implementation planning analysis rather than the technical aspects of IT project implementation. It identifies what needs to be done within the organization pre-implementation to increase a project's probability of success. The formulation of these understandings has been derived from investigations into the outcomes of IT projects and through analysis of many levels of implementation feedback to determine the root causes. Although these findings overlap to some degree, I have categorized them under the pre-investment decision-making and pre-implementation planning processes.

Both processes are interlinked by decisions that are made pre-investment, underpinning and driving the pre-implementation process that then cascades into how the project progresses through its life cycle. Because planning follows decision making, the actual decision-making process requires rigorous dissection and analysis. This is at the heart of corporate profiling. Profiling the organization pre-implementation and the disciplines involved in such profiling, is the conceptual idea of this book. The critical answers to why, how, and who are accountable will be analyzed thoroughly.

To fully discuss the technical and project management aspects of an IT project, the rebuttals from victims and liable parties, and the volumes of commentary that a failed IT project generates would create a substantial hole in the rain forest. I have therefore attempted to create a handbook and guide rather than yet another project management reference manual. With a strong background in IT and my research thesis in business, I will focus on the business level at which IT projects commence and also become unhinged.

# CHAPTER

# 1

# The Global Landscape of Failed IT Projects

*"I don't know the key to success, but the key to failure is trying to please everybody"*

Bill Cosby

## The Global Landscape of Failed IT Projects

O ngoing worldwide publicity surrounding major IT project failures highlights the considerable burden they cause to our economy and the financial and opportunity costs they incur for affected organizations. With businesses operating in an increasingly global, turbulent, competitive, and customer-driven environment, constant changes are required to adapt to this ever-morphing business milieu, which is driven by competition, profitability, costs, and customer demands.

With the latest global estimates putting the total direct and indirect costs of IT project failures at a staggering US$6.2 trillion (Ref: Roger Sessions). And with only one in three IT projects likely to be successfully delivered, one in four either failing or being cancelled, and the rest being "challenged" with massive budget overruns, its high time for a call to action by business leaders.

Major strategic IT investment decisions are fraught with risk and unknown outcomes. More importantly, such major changes have a cascading impact on an organization's processes, internal and external communications, and relationships, requiring each component also to adapt to these changes. Organizations that are unable or unwilling to match their changing environment and adapt their IT change programs accordingly will inevitably increase the probability of their IT project implementations failing to achieve their intended objectives. It follows, therefore, that to mitigate against the risk of systems becoming mismatched investment decisions, all aspects of proposed changes need to be rigorously managed with extreme precision before making any IT investment decisions.

During my many conversations and interviews with organizations that (for obvious reasons) demanded anonymity, one theme always emerged. Small, medium, and large organizations alike lamented their "shortfalls" that, with hindsight, became glaringly obvious. They all concurred that foresight into these areas could have been achieved if they had commissioned corporate profiling, as I described it to them, before they spent their hard-earned money. Specifically, I discussed with them the organizational decisions and processes they could have identified, analyzed, defined, and executed before making their investment decisions. In hindsight, they would have identified and consulted with their departments, staff, and end-users in the initiation process, well ahead of the project startup phase.

They unanimously concluded that their project failures were not due primarily to shortcomings in technology or to their organization's lack of technical knowledge, but rather because of inadequately shared and communicated strategies, a lack of pertinent input from unidentified indirect sources, communications which extend to include direct and indirect channels, insufficient training, and poor management practices. Since these are the likely factors at the crux of most organizational

## The Global Landscape of Failed IT Projects

IT implementation issues, why then, after millions of dollars have been spent on corporate strategic plans, mandating communication strategies and management training, do IT implementation projects still fail?

Whilst I completely agree that the above-mentioned investments, activities, and management practices need to be rigorously addressed throughout a project's life cycle, organizations that have such frameworks in place to support IT change will continue to experience project failures if they rely on these processes in isolation as a panacea for overcoming IT mismatches.

My research indicates that when only a single change process is applied to an entire IT project or, worse still, when multiple disparate change processes are used in isolation, they offer only a limited opportunity to successfully manage the entire IT implementation process from beginning to end. Considering that an IT implementation project involves extensive organizational change, a more comprehensive and integrated end-to-end pre-implementation change process is required.

# CHAPTER

# 2

# The IT Project Crisis that Won't Go Away

*"It has become appallingly obvious that our technology has exceeded our humanity"*

Albert Einstein

## The IT Project Crisis that Won't Go Away

Our ability to grasp and conceptualize new technologies and their benefits far exceeds our ability to comprehend the complexities of actually implementing technologies to meet these business needs. This is where our dreams end and our problems begin. What organizations need to fully comprehend is that it is not the technology itself that is at risk of failing, but it is the businesses themselves that put their projects at risk.

Ask yourself how there can be so many vendors out there who are so incompetent in their areas of expertise? And why there are so many inadequate software packages? The answers are that these vendors are not incompetent and the software packages are not inadequate. QED. Although it's easy to blame the software, in my studies and interviews with many companies that have experienced IT project failures, not once was the software to blame. And rarely, if ever, was the vendor incompetent. They were merely delivering what their customers asked for. IT implementation problems stem from a lack of corporate profiling practices—or, to put it more simply, a lack of extensive internal and external analysis to accurately identify and define business and user requirements before proceeding with an IT project.

All organizations expect their IT projects to go according to plan, to be delivered within budget and on time, and to deliver the agreed benefits. And the management of these organizations would be overjoyed if the final outcome exceeded their expectations. Why then, do so many organizations fail to rigorously plan their mission-critical pre-implementation process? And why do executives abdicate from their critical project decisions and responsibilities?

You will be amazed at how many IT project disasters have occurred simply because one or two people insisted on a course of action that was flawed or who inaccurately deemed their requirements to be accurate and comprehensive. When executives of an organization allow this situation to occur, the impact of project failures will not be realized until well after implementation has commenced or, worse still, supposedly completed. In short, an organization needs to be certain that what it is asking of its project accurately and comprehensively describes what the organization requires and not just what some parties think (or hope) will satisfy the organization's business needs.

Since IT implementations occur within complex and dynamic environments that involve many ambiguous factors, the cause and effect relationships are often difficult to identify and recognize. The reason why no single cause for failure can be identified after the event is because unknown cofactors, causative influences, unidentified situations, and the like are dynamically interrelated. This complex interrelation causes a chain of events that is impossible to unravel once the IT project has been declared a failure. However, if organizations are more rigorous and analytical in deciding pre-investment and pre-implementation the 'What,' 'Why,' 'How,' and 'When' of their project requirements, many of the subsequent contributing factors are likely to be eliminated.

Consider what happens when projects fail. In most cases, the vendors or those who implement the systems are held accountable, but the root cause of such failures could and should have been identified and eliminated at the very outset before any commitments to the project were made.

So how are these disasters avoided?

The key to avoiding an IT project disaster is to consider the factors outlined in this book from a pre-IT investment decision perspective rather than relying on project management skills to address rapidly emerging requirements and challenging problems. It is when requirements start to change and new requirements emerge that Project Managers become the project "firefighters," in an attempt to avert a looming disaster. Project managers do what the organizations task them to do. So, if an organization has not been precise or thorough enough in its preliminary instructions or planning, but still has high expectations of what will be delivered, the result could be a lose-lose situation in which the real cause of the failure cannot be identified. In fact, very rarely (if ever) is there any single cause for an IT project failure. But please be warned: there is also no "10-point plan" or easy path that guarantees an IT project's success. Corporate profiling creates the pre-implementation plan, but the process still needs to be effectively managed. The process won't work if the organization doesn't work at it.

> *Corporate Profiling* is a pre-investment decision-making process that identifies all pivotal project decisions that need to be made, communications and requirements sources, common processes, and interconnected links between internal and external parties to ensure all necessary input to projects occurs when needed. Ref: Wikipedia.

A vital issue often overlooked during IT investment decision making is that once vendors or system implementers have been selected and accountabilities assigned to the respective parties, the opportunity to identify critical factors covered under corporate profiling is lost. Corporate profiling must be done ahead of the investment decision, otherwise organizations lose the opportunity to identify and influence the all-important interconnected links between internal and external parties and to establish the necessary communications processes.

The resulting incomplete and inaccurate requirements that ensue from a premature investment decision will inevitably lead to project scope creep and ongoing revisions that contribute to project overruns and incomplete or missing functionality in the final production system. Without early corporate profiling, managing IT implementation after all parties (vendors and systems implementers) have been selected is a high-risk option to be avoided at all costs.

This book will assist organizations successfully identify and analyze business needs and user requirements when contemplating investing in IT systems. It will also help businesses ensure that production systems are supported and adopted by executives, internal and external users, customers, and stakeholders.

# CHAPTER

# 3

# Insight, Foresight, and Hindsight

*"Before everything else, getting ready is the secret of success"*
Henry Ford

## Starting with a Vision

Good IT projects start with a clear vision of their corporate direction, proceed with a collaborative decision, start with a comprehensive plan, and conclude with the desired outcomes.

Bad IT projects start with a decision, proceed with caution, and conclude with a hunt for scapegoats!

Evidence has clearly and repeatedly demonstrated that the difference between good IT projects and bad ones is determined by the extent to which an organization plans and executes pre-implementation processes.

If an organization is contemplating embarking on an IT project, its management needs to ask itself whether it is preparing for success or for failure.

## That Dreaded Feeling

Once a project is underway, organizations are past the point of no return and are no longer able to return to the planning phase. It is imperative therefore, that agreement must be reached on what needs to be done during a project, what else is required, and who is responsible for what aspects before the project commences. It is most unwise to make or change decisions and requirements during development or implementation because this is highly likely to create serious ramifications with destabilizing and disruptive consequences. If project requirements are not firmly established up front, change processes are not put in place, and people are not made accountable for input and decisions at the outset of the project, system changes will inevitably be required, resulting in the dreaded scope-creep. So, what can project sponsors do when they get that sinking feeling that an IT project is heading into troubled waters?

The following is not uncommon:

They consider the worst-case scenario but it's too ghastly to contemplate—how do they work their way out of the dilemma? Jobs are on the line! They imagine the stakeholder fallout and PR disaster of a failed project and their predictable "knee-jerk" reaction is to start looking for a likely scapegoat.

## The Light Bulb Comes On and the Big Aha!

Think, think, think! That's when they get the big Aha! They think to themselves, and then they start apportioning blame: "Well the software's been full of bugs from day one. We've lost numerous project days unscrambling programmers' mess-ups and design problems. How could we have trusted these programmers and their software? Phew, that was easy—just blame the software and the vendor. Simple!"

## The Reality of IT Projects and Software

In reality, software glitches and programming errors, to varying degrees, are pretty much a given. They can be disruptive to the point of creating disasters but are seldom if ever the root cause of IT project failures or software mismatches.

At the root of calamitous IT project failures are a lack of communications, poorly defined or inadequate user requirements, and insufficient consultation with all the appropriate end-users; such failures are rarely caused by poor quality work by project design and programming staff or programming and design errors.

Consider the many media headlines you've read reporting multi-million/billion-dollar IT implementation overruns that are still years from completion and the massive problems they raise for stakeholders and customers. Unless you are Microsoft Corporation, with millions of captive Windows® users and a multi-billion dollar Windows Vista® budget, your organization, like most others, cannot hope to survive many years of project and budget overruns.

## Executives' Role in IT Project Failures

When senior executives realize an IT project is over budget or over deadline with overpromised and under-delivered functionality, they will invariably be all over their vendors, system implementers, project managers, and CIOs (or CTOs).

This is the likely attitude of C-Level executives and company presidents when an IT implementation goes askew. It is only once the implementation is in progress or "supposedly" completed that they realize their system is mismatched or under-delivered. At this stage, finger pointing and "scapegoating" consumes valuable resources in a futile attempt to uncover how, why, or where in the implementation process the project went awry, and who is to blame. This is a futile exercise because they are only able to analyze the consequences not the root causes, which are often lost because of a lack of proper preparation and management accountability before the project started. Nevertheless, they still incorrectly blame third parties postmortem. Unfortunately, experience and history indicate that organizations typically see vendors, project managers, and CIOs as the obvious parties responsible for under-delivered and overbudget IT projects.

In truth, responsibility for under-delivered and overbudget IT projects lies predominantly with C-Level and senior executives, presidents, and managers themselves. These top-level decision makers often fail to profile their organizations at the outset of their projects to correctly identify organizational objectives, business needs, and sources for user and project requirements. When projects go askew, these executives should instead be examining whether their IT investment and project decision was underanalyzed, underscoped, undersupported, undercommunicated, or undertrained. Without a corporate profile to help identify and analyze these factors, they merely have an "overview" of their organizations and are bound to miss crucial elements and requirements for their projects.

The trap executives and managers consistently fall into is due to the relative investment size, level of importance, and the publicity surrounding the relevant project. As a result, they almost always task themselves with defining their organizational, business, user, and IT requirements up front. The mistake they make is to assume they have an extensive understanding of their organization's requirements. Consequently, they approve their projects without gathering extensive and accurate requirements or considering broader causal factors.

# Insight, Foresight, and Hindsight

It is therefore paradoxical that the "I'm over" statements come from those who prematurely authorize projects. What is an executive team thinking when it asks for IT project requirements from C-Level executives and managers, rather than pertinent end-users? The overall project requirements must include all internal user and business requirements as well as those of upstream and downstream customers and suppliers. These requirements can be obtained only from the actual users and departments and not from people who "claim" to know what their users' requirements are.

Because the roles of senior executives are strategic and not operational, they simply do not have the necessary insight into the deep-rooted internal and external organizational relationships that define their organization's profile. This is not to say that they don't know their business. However, their senior roles often diminish the view of their organization's formal and informal processes and inter-connected relationships, all of which can be either internal or external to the organization. Identifying these are vital first steps in being able to identify channels and sources for project communications and requirements before scoping, selecting vendors, and making project commitments. These causal factors, inter-connected relationships, processes, and requirements can only be fully identified from a comprehensive corporate profile. Not identifying these factors is often a major contributing factor to IT project failures.

Knowing how an organization operates and identifying strategic requirements is vastly different from being able to identify the elements within a corporate profile and how they feed into, and impact upon, the outcomes of IT projects.

# Stop Blaming the Software

## Post-implementation Discovery

Analysis of the final consequences and outcomes of failed IT projects does not bring one any closer to determining what factors, prior to investing in systems, would have contributed to more accurate decisions about the organization's real needs.

However, identifying, analyzing, and understanding the root causes of failures will greatly assist future implementations.

Consequently, what organizations need before going down the IT investment decision path is insight into their requirements, rather than hindsight when a project is derailed by poor planning up front. Organizational insight as well as hindsight from previous projects will provide the foresight for an organization's future implementations. Hindsight is only beneficial if people can learn from it.

If an organization can objectively answer the following questions at the conclusion of an implementation it will at least be one step ahead of most other organizations.

(1) Was the IT investment decision under-decided and under-supported by presidents, senior managers and C-Level executives prior to making the initial IT investment?

(2) Was the chosen solution under-adopted by end users because they felt their requirements and input were not required?

(3) Was the solution under-supported by vendors or developers because it was not their primary business function?

(4) Were the implementation processes under-governed by the organization's governance framework?

(5) Was the project under-funded by the CFO, between business units or the organization?

(6) Did the organization underestimate the critical role corporate profiling plays in the pre-investment stage of IT projects?

These factors require attention and action before project commitments are made because once a project has commenced it's too late to influence any of these factors.

The other key question vendors and customers should be asking is, "Did we assume extensive requirements were collected and correctly documented from the most pertinent and pivotal parties?" Most of the time, both parties automatically assume requirements gathering has been diligently executed. Often, it is precisely this assumption that sets the stage for the derailment of a project.

# CHAPTER

# 4

# Scapegoating

*"A good scapegoat is nearly as welcome as a solution to the problem"*

Author unknown

# Scapegoating

## Gearing Up for Failure

At the outset of a project, vendors, developers, and systems implementers assume that their customer has meticulously and extensively gathered and documented the organization's complete and accurate project requirements. The customer also assumes that their IT, business, and user requirements have been diligently gathered and correctly documented. Otherwise, why embark upon the project?

Frequently, both parties later discover rather that their project's requirements are incomplete or incorrect. The primary reasons for insufficient, inaccurate, or incomplete requirements are because either the wrong people have been tasked with specifying the requirements or because they failed to gather requirements from pivotal and often unidentified user sources. These sources, invariably, can often only be properly identified through corporate profiling.

Additionally, vendors, developers, and systems implementers fall prey of their own self-interest. Inadvertently they exacerbate the problem by pushing organizations to start the project prematurely. This in itself becomes a double-edged sword since there is a fine line between what their customer deems acceptable or unacceptable in terms of paying for additional project changes once implementation is underway.

This scenario is largely dependent upon the size of the customer's organization and whether the customer is able to absorb the additional costs needed to continue with the implementation. If changes or scope-creep increase the project's budget beyond its established limits, the project may fail or need to be euthanized. This inevitably reflects badly upon vendors, developers, and systems implementers and makes them the prime target for becoming third-party scapegoats. Why? Because, inevitably, the customer will deflect the blame for the project's failure onto someone else.

In the final analysis, irrespective of how failed projects are rationalized, heads will roll and scapegoats will be found. These pitfalls are easily avoided if all parties involved insist on comprehensive corporate profiling before implementing the project.

## The Art of Seeking out Scapegoats

Let it be said upfront: there is no single or absolute definition of what constitutes a "failed IT project." However, the vast majority of implementation failures are identified and defined when the project goes over budget, is overdue, or is not fully utilized by the user because the new system does not deliver the anticipated benefits or functionality the organization requested from its suppliers or vendors.

# Scapegoating

When IT implementations become rogue, runaway projects or fail to deliver, organizations generally demand that scapegoats:

(1) Take the blame so the company doesn't look inept in the eyes of its stakeholders
(2) So it doesn't look technically or commercially incompetent
(3) It doesn't appear that the company made poor decisions
(4) Take the blame for cost overruns

As with any major IT implementation, everyone is responsible for his or her contribution to the project, and ultimately someone will be accountable for poor outcomes. Unfortunately, in this context, accountability is synonymous with scapegoat because someone or some third party (or parties) will be forced to shoulder the blame for corporate accountability to the organization and its stakeholders.

Typically, such accountability will rest on the shoulders of those most closely involved, such as:

- The CIO
- The departmental IT Manager
- The project sponsor
- The project manager

With accountability attributed to the appropriate internal scapegoat, the "Root Cause" will then be further analyzed and will ultimately be pinned on external third party scapegoats such as:

- The vendor
- The developer or systems implementer
- The software
- Third-party consultants and project managers

Ultimately, one of the above internal and or external entities will shoulder the blame for IT projects failing. This will inevitably result in a public fall from grace, being fired, being blacklisted, or the supplier, systems implementer or consulting agency's name becoming a "Chinese Whisper" on the notorious industry rumor-mill, which will seriously impact future demand for the company's products and services.

This is not to say that a bloodbath always ensues, but my involvement in numerous postmortem committees suggests that this is generally the rule rather than the exception. Often the blame for project problems is attributed either to internal people who are tasked with implementing systems, or to third-party suppliers, rather than the C-Level executives, managers, and presidents who prematurely gave the go-ahead in the first place.

## Why Third Parties become Scapegoats

So, why do other people and third parties become scapegoats when executive decision makers are responsible for the parameters guiding most projects? Often it is due to the time lag between a unilateral IT investment decision and the project's completion or failure point. If the time differential is protracted, executive decision makers conveniently forget that it was they who made investment and project decisions with insufficient input or feedback from the rest of the organization regarding the requirements for a successful outcome.

This time lag causes people to incorrectly assume that subsequent project problems that adversely affected the project's outcome are caused by more recent events, rather than as a result of decisions made before the commencement of the project. Accountability and blame are therefore attributed to those involved in the actual project implementation, rather than those who made the investment and pre-implementation decisions in the first place.

To avoid this situation and to ensure a rigorous pre-IT implementation decision-making process, corporate profiling must be undertaken. If not, memory of the pre-implementation process will be impaired or steered by a myopic vision of those really responsible for it. The end result is that those who were responsible will not be held accountable for their all-important premature investment and flawed decisions in the pre-IT implementation process.

## Identifying the Unidentifiable

It is said that theologians are experts in the unknown. Likewise, organizations need to be experts at identifying "unknown contributing factors" that will underpin the success or failure of their IT implementations. These factors are easily missed because, unless one knows where to look for them, they will remain obscure and unidentifiable.

These factors often appear as minutiae in the big picture (and are assumed to be too obvious to be overlooked), or are so well hidden in the corporate scaffolding that they are unidentifiable. Alternatively, they may be so simple that they are simply ignored or mismanaged. Murphy's Law always catches people out when they least expect it to.

Only once an organization has been extensively profiled can it possibly hope to identify all the factors that need to be considered. This profile will help organizations identify and understand the level of detail required in the end-to-end implementation process. However minute or insignificant certain components in the process are believed to be, these are often the components that determine whether an IT implementation succeeds or fails.

This means that when considering an IT implementation, organizations and their people need to be able to identify, manage, execute, and check every step in the pre-implementation process. This will ensure that no corporate relationships are unidentified, no information sources are left untapped, no communications channels are unidentified, decisions will be supported, and that no requirements will be left unasked for and undocumented before project commitments are made.

The pre-implementation process is a self-contained process that most organizations unfortunately tend not to embrace as fervently as they do the implementation itself. Nevertheless, it is a process that must be adopted and effectively managed to achieve a successful implementation.

In making a major personal investment in property, stock, or a new car, we need to make a detailed analysis of all the factors that may impact positively or negatively upon such an investment. Similarly, in making IT investment decisions, analyzing the details is paramount because, as always, the devil is in the detail. What may at first appear to be a minor detail can quickly become a major factor in determining a project's success or failure.

# CHAPTER

# 5

# Where and How IT Project Problems Begin

*"It is wise to direct your anger towards problems—not people; to focus your energies on answers—not excuses"*
William Arthur Ward

# Where and How IT Project Problems Begin

T o understand the many possible reasons for IT implementations going askew, we need to review events at the inception of these projects, rather than analyzing problematic outcomes.

Based on research into the causes of IT project failures, it is evident many organizations do not make their pre-implementation IT project decisions within rigorous frameworks. This is why IT failures are often caused by poor communications, a lack of support, and changing requirements that can all be traced back to poor decision making at the outset.

The starting point of any IT project is the investment decision. However, this decision must first be supported by an extensive, rigorous, and collaborative pre-implementation decision-making process. All too often IT investment decisions are made in semi-isolation by senior executives without the crucial input of relevant business units, departments, stakeholders, or employees. This results in project disparities before the implementation has even begun. Or, worse still, the decision is made in isolation immediately before outsourcing to third parties, thereby allowing subsequent critical project decisions to be made *adhoc* by external parties.

# Stop Blaming the Software

## Decision making and Accountability

If the pre-implementation decision-making process is either not established or lacks structure and rigor, these decisions will be insubstantial, with a lack of accountability for outcomes. It is also unlikely executives, managers, stakeholders, and users will support these decisions.

It is therefore imperative that a pre-implementation decision-making process is established to ensure a solid framework for all subsequent project decisions. These decisions need accountability for reasons and actions by the 'Who,' 'Why,' 'When,' and 'How' of projects.

Up front this framework will ensure that accountability is assigned for fundamental decisions and that each decision is grounded in planning and strategy rather than based on flimsy reasons. Before these decisions are made, management needs to address the following questions:

- Why are we investing in this IT system?
- Will the system help us achieve our strategic objectives and vision?
- Is our business aligned with our IT strategies?
- What is our communications strategy for the project?
- How and who will manage our communications?
- How will we gain and preserve project support?
- Who will be responsible and accountable for project requirements?
- What metrics will we use to determine the project's success and are these metrics aligned with our strategic objectives?

- How will we ensure the involvement of all pertinent parties and particularly end users?
- What strategies do we have in place to ensure successful user adoption?

All too often C-Level executives make investment decisions with little or no collaboration and then direct their staff to "make it happen" (with predictably poor project outcomes). Alternatively, the IT investment decision is made and then by virtue of association and credibility with the Executive Office, external consultants are appointed to make decisions on behalf of an organization. In both cases, collaboration at peer level and with other departments is overlooked.

This creates another scenario and a set of alternative reasons for unaccountable and isolated decisions. This happens where the people making the investment or project decisions have either the authority, expertise, or power to edify themselves and their decisions. Others, therefore, do not feel obligated to contribute or voice their opinions or are not even involved in the final decision making. In this case, no-one questions the individual or parties who make the decisions. This is not an uncommon scenario and is more prevalent than organizations care to admit.

To avoid the above situation, the decision-making process must be rigorously profiled to identify the appropriate people to be included in the decision-making process as well as the departments or business units that will be affected by the new system. In devolving responsibility and accountability to appropriate parties, the opportunity for a single person assuming total control of all decision making is eliminated. The most appropriate individuals then become fully accountable for their independent decisions, thereby improving the quality of their team's input, as opposed to groups being loosely and collectively responsible.

Alternatively, when everyone is made responsible with no accountability, less care is taken because there are no consequences for their actions.

By undertaking profiling, the outcome is tripartite:

- The group-think effect is less likely to occur because people have ownership and accountability for their input
- People cannot make off-the-cuff decisions without having to bear the consequences at a later date
- The pre-implementation decision-making process becomes structured, rigorous, and collaborative.

Since IT implementations are often drawn out processes, time often erodes the memory of who actually owned the decision and who was accountable for the quality of the input into the decision. Time is also the master of revolving corporate doors where responsibilities and accountabilities can come and go over the period of an IT project. For this reason, accountability needs to be preserved by being reassigned as and when organizational changes occur.

## Requirements and Input

The other major cause of IT implementation problems is incomplete business requirements and user input. An organization may have a general idea of its requirements, and may also have sound business reasons for a project commencing as soon as possible. However, business objectives may not be aligned across departments and may also not support corporate strategy.

Where this is the case, it is likely for an organization to request IT systems to be implemented without knowing specifically what it really expects or needs the new systems to deliver. This often comes about because the requirements or decisions for the IT investment have not been thoroughly identified or analyzed, and are, therefore, not nearly specific enough. If an IT investment and commitments are made at this early stage of a project, before extensive and thorough requirements have been identified, some degree of failure or, at worst, a complete disaster is inevitable.

The foundation of a successful new IT project is organizational communications, business and user-specific requirements, and executive, user and stakeholder support and input. An accurate and fully supported investment decision cannot be made without all these elements being present. Even if an organization has what appears to be an extensive document specifying the requirements of the project process, it is unlikely to be complete without critical input from all the relevant parties who should be involved. More often than not, requirements are not clearly identified because pivotal input from internal users, customers, and suppliers is not sought or even identified as a critical business requirement.

## Compounding the Problem—Winning the Business

The problem is compounded when vendors and service providers win the business. The following two scenarios are commonly encountered:

# Stop Blaming the Software

Scenario one is where vendors unwittingly believe their customers know precisely what they want and need from the system and that what has been specified is an accurate and complete requirements document that scopes exactly what should be included. Vendors aim to stick to the requirements document and deliver to specification without variations or increases in scope. This is important because they have based their quotations, estimates, and resources on the specifications.

The second scenario is where, having already decided on an IT system, an organization appoints an external consultant or consulting agency and delegates requirements gathering to them. This is problematic because an external party cannot possibly know or identify another organization's needs and requirements as intimately as its own employees can. This lack of organizational intimacy and understanding will reduce the quality and extensiveness of the requirements that are identified.

Moreover, in the absence of a corporate profile, the requirements are unlikely to be fully defined or extensive enough to include those hidden and less obvious requirements. Consequently, as the project progresses, the requirements specification document will continually morph and expand as additional requirements continue to be identified during the implementation process.

Over time these "minor must-have" changes and emerging "new" requirements often conflict with the original specifications, and accommodating these changes introduces scope-creep into the project.

# Where and How IT Project Problems Begin

## Compounding the Problem—Changing Requirements and Scope-Creep

Project scopecreep is synonymous with overbudget and overtime and, unchecked, it can result in a runaway project. This is usually an indication of either inadequately sourced business or user requirements, an IT-driven rather than a business-driven project, or unintentional incrementalism. These can all lead a project to the point of diminishing returns, where the project's viability itself becomes questionable.

Minor changes are inevitable, but not to the extent that they result in a complete project overhaul that bears no resemblance to the original item. This is why change requests must be managed and monitored through a rigorous change—control process. Even apparently minor changes can impact a project in a major way, due to either the cascading effect from integrating with other systems (or applications) or previously unidentified user requirements. Profiling before starting a project will identify interlinked processes to determine who is accountable for individual requirements. This eliminates the need for subsequent changes because requirements are correctly identified at the outset.

Continually changing and evolving specifications are often a major source of consultant and vendor revenue – all at the customer's expense for not having profiled the requirements at the outset.

The onus is equally on "trusted" vendors to rigorously ensure that when customers accept their business, they have undertaken corporate profiling. By ensuring that their clients have undertaken corporate profiling up front, they can be assured they will have fully specified, accurate, and extensive requirements, thereby minimizing the potential for them to become the next scapegoat. Obviously, vendors will want to write up the business as early as possible but it's ultimately not in their or their clients' best interests to contribute to an IT project failure by having a premature project start.

Later in this book I will discuss the vendor—and solution-selection process as key elements in decision making. It is certainly a decision that is easier to make once an organization has been profiled and has a clear understanding of what its needs and requirements are.

# CHAPTER

# 6

# Factors Contributing to IT Project Failures

*"Most people spend more time and energy going around problems than in trying to solve them"*

Henry Ford

# Factors Contributing to IT Project Failures

A common contributing factor for IT project failures is often due to disparate processes between an organization's functions or departments and fragmented communications between executives, managers, and the rest of the organization.

These disparities result in *adhoc* decision making, differing and conflicting requirements, poor communications, a lack of project support and an unclear understanding of the project's objectives. These are, however, merely symptoms of the problem that can often be linked directly back to either a lack of unaccountability for decisions or poor decision-making processes at executive levels. By undertaking corporate profiling, critical decisions organizations' leaders and executives need to make at their project's outset become glaringly obvious.

By ensuring decisions are based on factual and comprehensive organizational requirements, an organization's profile will provide the foundation upon which to make sound IT investment decisions. A corporate profile will also highlight areas of weaknesses, alerting the organization to actions that need to be taken pre-implementation rather than "firefighting" during or after the project is complete. Similarly, it will also emphasize the organization's key areas of strength that can be leveraged to full advantage. Finally, it elucidates where more collaboration and cohesion across an organization is required in order to mitigate disparities.

## Categories, Disciplines, and Causal Factors

Interviews with organizations during my research revealed the following causal factors within each discipline as the most prominent contributors to IT implementation failures. The causal factors that emerged from each discipline provided an insight into the dynamic nature of IT implementations and of different individual perceptions of the situation and reasons for their implementations failure.

| Category | Discipline | Causal factors |
|---|---|---|
| Organization | Communication | • No communications strategy <br> • Lack of communications <br> • Only downward directed communication |
| Management | Decision making | • No decision-making criteria <br> • Unsolicited user input <br> • Poor user interface design |
| IT | IT Governance | • Under investment in systems or business training |

Most of these causal factors indicate the absence of rigor in an organization's pre-implementation decision-making processes. These causal factors also reflect the lack of strategic project decisions being made by executives. Such decisions that need to be made at senior level require organizational visibility, collective input, collaboration, accountability, and support.

# Factors Contributing to IT Project Failures

## Organizational and Leadership Factors that will Increase IT Project Success

The pivotal organizational and leadership decisions that need to be addressed in order to increase the probability of a project's success are:

- A firm commitment to the investment decision by the organization, its stakeholders, and executives
- Clearly articulated organizational strategy and objectives
- Clearly defined success metrics
- Best-fit vendor, system implementer, and solution selection
- The quality, validity, and extent of project requirement sources
- Extensively secured support and commitment for the project from the entire organization, including end users
- The pace at which the implementation will occur
- The extent of project scoping and planning
- Structural variables such as budget, time-frame, and success measures
- Communications between IT, management, the organization, vendors, the external value chain, and users
- Organizational commitment to, and readiness for, change
- Correlation between project complexity, IT skills, and knowledge base

These actions and decisions alone will substantially reduce the risk of an IT mismatch since the success of the implementation will be determined by them.

Support, commitment, requirements, communications, and the skill set of vendors are commonly overlooked factors

## Stop Blaming the Software

because people incorrectly believe IT implementations are purely technical projects for IT to manage. However, it is the sociological factors that will more often than not determine a project's success rather than the technology itself.

Profiling effectively pinpoints the 'who with,' 'where from,' 'when,' and 'how' of these factors, thereby reducing the risk of them being overlooked or poorly conducted due to a lack of information and organizational visibility.

## Sequence of Events Driving the Implementation Process

All IT implementations should encompass a sequence of events and a plan to drive projects to successful conclusions.

The following planning stages of the pre-implementation process are underpinned by disciplines that will later be unbundled.

(1)  Begin with a conclusive organizational decision

(2)  Start with the support of all stakeholders

(3)  Be supported by organizational strategies

(4)  Proceed with clear communications channels

(5)  Put IT risk and governance measures in place

(6)  Monitor the quality and progress of the project and celebrate successes along the way

(7)  Incorporate a plan for organizational change management

(8)  Include a continuous input and feedback mechanism

(9)  Ensure appropriate training for all system users

(10) Conclude with full user adoption and success metrics appraisal

## Factors Contributing to IT Project Failures

Close scrutiny will reveal that in the case of most failed IT projects, one or more of the above steps will have been poorly executed or overlooked entirely.

Simply put, an IT project will be at risk if the entire organization does not follow and support the above path. This path encompasses organizational and project disciplines that require the full participation of all parties to achieve a successful outcome.

Instead of wasting time seeking out scapegoats for a failed IT project, organizations should rather adopt the steps and pivotal disciplines that need to be rigorously established and executed pre-implementation and which are critical to reducing the risk of project failures.

This is achieved by unbundling an organization into categories, functions, processes, external value chain relationships, and the pre-implementation process into steps and disciplines. This will make an organization's elements more visible, allowing it to identify and gain a better understanding of where each discipline needs to be applied and profiled. Unbundling will also identify gaps within an organization's decision-making and pre-implementation processes, where they are exposed, and whether or not corrective action needs to be taken.

# CHAPTER
# 7

# Corporate
# Profiling

*"The beginning is the most important part of the work"*
Plato

# Corporate Profiling

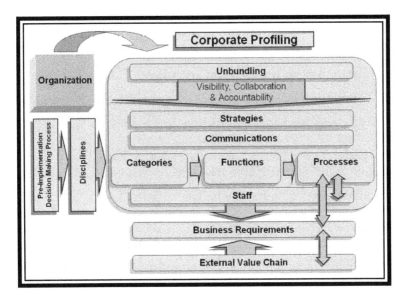

C orporate profiling promotes three key principles: Visibility, Collaboration, and Accountability.

Visibility of an organization's key elements is vital to the profiling process and can only be achieved once an organization has been unbundled or dissected.

Profiling promotes collaboration on all strategic decisions to ensure that unbiased quality decisions are arrived at, consensus is achieved, and decisions are fully supported. Collaboration is also a prerequisite for requirements gathering.

Accountability empowers employees to drive change and to feel involved rather than becoming cynical or resistant to change. Accountability is also a critical factor for ensuring quality input into strategic project decisions.

Corporate profiling is a relatively straightforward yet comprehensive process and is the first step to be undertaken before an organization even contemplates investing in an IT system. Profiling will dramatically reduce the risk of an IT failure at the outset because it establishes a solid foundation of qualified, objective, comprehensive, and accurate organizational information from the appropriate sources.

The information derived from a corporate profile provides the answers and input required for each step within the pre-implementation framework. This greatly helps to ensure that each fundamental step has rigor and accountability locked in rather than being left to chance.

By integrating this information into the pre-implementation process no interconnected corporate relationships are left unidentified and no information sources are left untapped. Decisions are made, executed, and fully supported and no requirements are left undocumented when embarking on the critical path of implementing an IT system.

Profiling will significantly improve the identification of internal and external business, user, and stakeholder requirements. This is achieved by recognizing that causal factors are often indirect or unidentified and that the source of such salient requirements can either be external or deeply hidden within an organization. In the process, profiling identifies those internal or external factors that may be resistant to change, making ongoing management tasks more effective in countering such resistance.

## Corporate Profiling Identifies

- Where systems, processes, relationships, and people are interlinked within an organization and its external and internal value chain
- The common or causal factors between corporate, business, and IT
- Hidden or not so obvious factors that could easily be overlooked

# Corporate Profiling

Corporate profiling consists of two phases:

Phase one delivers an in-depth blueprint of an organization, its functions, processes, people, and their interlinked relationships. Each organizational element is either directly or indirectly and formally or informally involved in the change. In addition, these elements will either positively or negatively influence other elements that may impact on the success or failure of a project.

Phase two analyzes an organization's external value chain of upstream suppliers and downstream customers. Once they have been identified, their relationships with the organization can be analyzed to determine whether they are direct or indirect and formal or informal to identify where they are interlinked with the organization, its functions, processes, and people.

## What does Corporate Profiling Achieve?

The three key principles of profiling, visibility, collaboration, and accountability help ensure that profiling:

(1) Unbundles an organization to provide visibility of all of its functions, departments, and processes as well as its customers and suppliers that will impact, effect, or need to be involved in the IT implementation.

(2) Identifies the interconnected relationships and links between an organization's functions, departments, tasks, and its customers and suppliers.

(3) Identifies which internal and external information sources need to be involved in requirements gathering. These are often the people or departments that liaise with customers at a grassroots or coal-face level or even informally.

(4) Identifies all direct and indirect, internal and external, formal and informal communications channels and sources.

(5) Establishes and supports the correct and most efficient communication channels between parties involved in the project. This is inclusive of the organization, its customers, suppliers, vendors, and stakeholders.

(6) Provides an extensive framework of salient decisions and questions that an organization's leaders and executives need to address at the outset. These decisions validate the project and underpin its success by mandating core strategies vital for the project's execution and flow. Consequently, these decisions require collaboration between relevant parties and peers to ensure consensus, and therefore a fully supported decision.

(7) Ensures commonality between the organization, business, and IT strategies and end objectives and ensures that these are clearly and effectively communicated and understood by all parties.

(8) Assigns decision making and responsibilities to appropriate people, groups, and departments and ensures simultaneously that ultimately only one person is accountable for each decision. This increases the probability that optimal decisions based upon factual, high-quality input are made. It reduces the "he said – she said" finger-pointing scenario and blind, off-the-cuff decision making that can occur when people do not feel involved or empowered.

(9) Ensures that the most appropriate organizational components and people are responsible and accountable for their input into the decision-making process. Often, when people are not made accountable for their decisions or actions, they blindly

follow or acquiesce either because they cannot be bothered deciding on the best course of action themselves or because they perceive the other person to be more knowledgeable.

All of the above will ensure that an organization's profile will be an extensive blueprint for what it needs to know, undertake, and establish before proceeding with an IT investment.

A comprehensive profile must be founded on common objectives between the three business categories (organization, management, and IT). Executive support from within these categories must be secured, and cohesion and collaboration must take place at all levels to drive tri-directional communications throughout an organization.

Since each category contributes to the development of an organization's operational, management, and pre-implementation processes, they are all involved in profiling and are the enablers of successful IT projects and ultimately will sustain future IT innovation.

Before committing vendors and system implementers to an IT project, organizations must invest time and effort upfront in developing a comprehensive corporate profile. Unless organizations can address each element within the profiling process before making their investment decisions, they will not be adequately prepared to move forward. Insights gained into the inextricable links between an organization's internal and external elements will give management the foresight of knowing precisely what their business, users, and customer IT system requirements are. Such insight will serve the organization far better before IT investment decisions are made, rather than after the project's conclusion.

# CHAPTER

# 8

# Unbundling the
# Organization

*"While intelligent people can often simplify the complex, a food is
more likely to complicate the simple"*
Gerald W. Grumet

# Unbundling the Organization

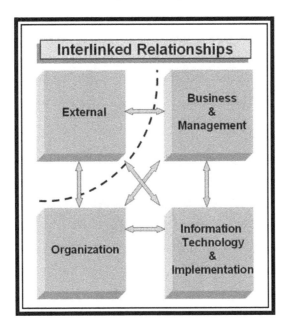

Although profiling does not include an analysis of competitors, industry, or government regulations, it is important to remember that the external environment is usually a major influence driving an organization's decision to invest in IT systems. Even though this environment may provide the impetus for change, it is internal organizational factors that contribute to IT implementation mismatches.

Organizations comprise three major categories, whose naming convention may vary from company to company. Such names will also depend on the size of their organization.

These categories are:

- Organizational or business
- Management
- Implementation or IT

## Stop Blaming the Software

These categories are then unbundled in order to identify the organization's individual components. Some organizations may be structured according to categories, functions, and processes and others according to functions, business units/departments, and processes. Once an organization's main components have been identified, it is easier to understand the relationship between an organization, its management, and IT. By further separating these components and their influencing factors, the many levels of complexity are also recognizable as well as the influence and impact these components have on one another.

## Unbundling the Organization

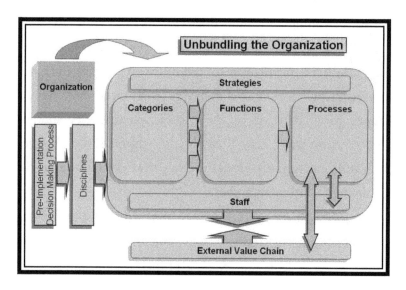

Corporate profiling works by peeling off the layers of an organization starting at the top (or outer layer) and working towards the center. The four primary layers of an organization are as follows:

# Unbundling the Organization

(1) The three categories of an organization must always be interconnected by a common strategy for communications, decision making, and process control to avoid dysfunctional and isolated "Silos" occurring within an organization.

(2) These strategies need to straddle every function and department or business unit, connecting them to an organization's goals and bottom-line objectives.

(3) Functions, departments or business units are connected by the processes in which they are involved, and each process is linked by the people involved. Since functional processes and regular learned tasks are documented as part of a job function, there is little risk of them being unidentified or overlooked. However, it is still imperative they are profiled so any disparities that may exist may be identified.

(4) The organization's position in the value chain will determine whether its processes extend to, or integrate with, suppliers, customers, both, or not at all.

Identifying all interconnected functions, departments, people, and processes is integral to a project's success. However obscure or indirect they are, they can often be a source of project requirements or will need to be solicited for their input and involvement in a project. Often, it is only the most immediately apparent interconnected points that are identified because they have a direct impact or influence on the project's requirements. This is particularly true where an organization appoints an inappropriate person or third party to source its business and user requirements. Identifying these interconnected points is vital to creating an accurate profile, and organizations need to be sure to identify interconnections with those on the less obvious external continuum as they are easily overlooked.

Thoroughly identifying interconnected points will ensure that all relevant people and departments are identified and become involved early in the project decision-making process. It will also ensure that effective communications with appropriate parties and people are established at a project's outset. Input, information, and requirements can thereby be solicited from all appropriate sources, which will prevent the common mistake of singling out only the obvious departments, people, or processes. Unmerited, intangible, and unqualified requirements sourced from a select few people or departments that unwittingly think they know the full and complete business scope and user requirements are a recipe for disaster.

With visibility and transparency concerning where and how departments, functions, processes, and people are interconnected, an organization's links and relationships will become apparent. The organization will then be able to determine whether the IT project will directly or indirectly influence or impact these parties. By identifying these cause-and-effect relationships before implementation, an organization is better equipped to fully comprehend the entire pre-implementation process and what is required for the successful implementation of the project.

Eighty percent of an iceberg is hidden beneath the water line. Similarly, the vast majority of project requirements are hidden. These not-so-obvious requirements need to be derived from the less apparent areas of the organization and its external value chain. It is important to realize that when sources of information and requirements are left unsolicited they will almost certainly adversely impact the project's success.

# Unbundling the Organization

## Profiling the Organization

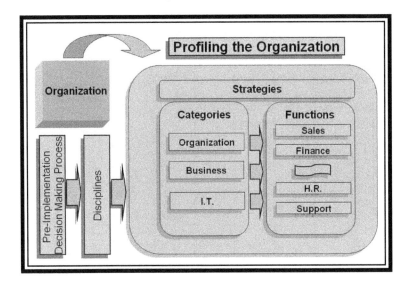

The type, size, and how a company is organized will determine its specific functions, business units and or departments.

### *Profiling Information for an Organization*

- o Define the organization's current corporate strategy in 40 words or less
- o What are its three organizational categories and what are their individual strategies?
- o Do the category strategies support its overall strategy?
- o Identify all business functions, business units, or departments—i.e.: Sales, HR, Finance, Operations, and IT.
- o Define objectives for each of the above
- o What are the individual strategies for each function, business, or department?
- o What is the organization's vision?

## Profiling Core Processes

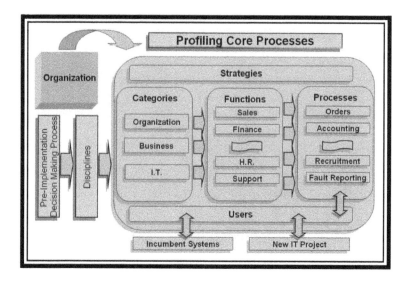

Once a decision to invest in new technology or a new IT system has been made, particularly for major projects such as corporate CRM or ERP systems, an organization needs to fully identify and understand how the system will impact upon or integrate into its core business processes. Since implementing any new IT system is not an isolated event affecting just a single business function or department, the organization needs to be collectively involved in the change process as the entire organization will be impacted. Profiling will help create a shift in an organization's mindset away from the perception that the implementation is a one-off or isolated event, but rather a process and facilitator for understanding how the organization operates as a whole.

To identify the points of process integration, an organization needs to determine what its current processes and systems are, how they envision them to be, and what needs to be done to achieve the desired outcomes. Using the profiling information from "Profiling Information for an Organization" as the starting point, they can begin to profile their core processes.

## *Profiling Information for Core Processes*

Identify all of the following:

o   All core business processes

o   All formal processes that each individual function, business unit, or department executes

o   All informal processes each function conducts—these are often manual or undocumented processes that have developed over time i.e. information sharing, paper forms for communicating between departments, or processing hand-written documents

o   The common or integrated processes between each function, business unit, or department

o   Where and what processes are integrated

o   Where and how incumbent processes can be made more efficient

o   What processes will become obsolete, which ones will be redesigned, which ones will stay the same and which ones will require integration with the new system or processes

o   Identify incumbent systems that may be impacted

o   What systems will become redundant with the introduction of the new system

o   Identify the common or interfacing systems between each function, business unit, or department

o   Any interfaces redundant systems have with other systems to ensure these are addressed in the requirements documents

## Stop Blaming the Software

Many organizations think in terms of business functions such as IT, HR, Accounting, Sales etc., rather than the actual processes they perform and how these processes are interconnected. When one interconnected process changes, it will very likely impact another process, which in turn will impact other processes, creating a ripple effect. This is why when an automated process relies on input from another manual process the automated process will often only be as efficient as the manual process (the overall process is only as strong as the weakest link). Therefore, most of an organization's incumbent intra-company processes need to be redesigned to a certain degree to ensure efficient processing, input, and integration into the new system and to match the strategic objectives.

Herein lies the big picture that (with the benefit of a corporate profile) organizations will then be able to identify where internal functions or departments are connected through common processes and where those processes are integrated with its customers or suppliers processes and systems. Linking the organization through processes or functions rather than by isolated departments encourages the pursuit of common goals, shared objectives, and actualization of the organization's "Big Picture" strategy. More importantly, it will also identify if, where, and how suppliers and customers integrate into the organization's incumbent IT systems, functions, departments, and processes. This will allow an organization to understand precisely how it will be impacted and what it needs to do to adapt to the change. It will also help the organization identify precisely where its user requirements must come from.

# Unbundling the Organization

## Unbundling the Pre-Implementation Process

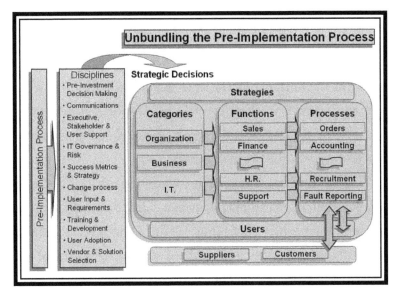

By unbundling the pre-implementation process we are able to break down each step into specific disciplines. These disciplines all require strategic decisions at the project's outset so they can be successfully established, managed, and adopted by the organization throughout the project's life cycle.

These disciplines include the following:

### Disciplines

(1) Pre-investment decision-making process
(2) Communications
(3) Executive, stakeholder, and user support
(4) IT governance and risk
(5) Success metrics and strategy
(6) Change process
(7) User input and requirements gathering
(8) Training and process development
(9) User adoption
(10) Vendor and solution selection

# Stop Blaming the Software

Poor execution of any one of these steps will be reflected in areas of weakness in one or more of these disciplines. By separating these disciplines into logical steps, organizations can analyze previous IT projects to identify what disciplines within the implementation process were deficient. Additionally, by pinpointing such weaknesses, the organization can determine whether the problem was the result of inadequate profiling or a lack of rigor at the project's outset.

Either way, it will assist in identifying which function, business unit, department, or group needs to adopt a more rigorous approach to managing certain disciplines. Generally, a lack of information or a generalized response from any of the departments or groups pertaining to any of these disciplines will indicate weaknesses.

Unbundling the pre-implementation process into separate disciplines provides a framework of strategic decisions that need to be made as well as identifying what needs to be profiled pre-implementation. As easy as it may seem to simply dissect or unbundle the organization and process into steps and disciplines, the ultimate success of each one depends upon the extent to which it is profiled and then adhered to pre-implementation.

## Organizational Decision-making Framework

This framework identifies the seminal decisions and actions the organization needs to undertake internally before proceeding with an IT investment. Each of these decisions is a step within the pre-implementation process that needs to be extensively profiled if they are to be effectively communicated and successfully managed. Although they are separated into spccific disciplines within the pre-implementation process, do not be fooled by this simplicity. They are all important decisions the organization needs to make.

Each discipline requires the Executive Team to make strategic decisions before IT investment and project commencement. The first of these disciplines to be profiled is 'pre-investment decision making.' If the organization does not have accountable and justifiable support for the decisions within each discipline, then it is unlikely to enjoy the full support of pertinent parties and stakeholders. It will also not be supported by an absolute and all-inclusive strategic plan to ensure the project's success. Strategic plans become operational objectives—they will not materialize without a strategy to support them.

(1)   **Pre-investment decision making**—Organizations need to carefully select who, how, what, and why parties will be involved in the investment decision and implementation. Always promote information transparency so the right information is available when needed to support optimal decision making. Also, be aware that various members of the organization have very different agendas that will influence the selection processes.

(2)   **Communications**—Develop an organizational communication strategy for employees, users, customers, suppliers, and stakeholders before implementation. This will help them understand how the new system will work and what changes will affect them. Asking for their input will also include them in the change proccss to support their 'buy in' to the project.

(3) **Executive, stakeholder, and user support**—Be sure to take all necessary steps to secure the support of stakeholders, executives, managers, and users before proceeding with an investment decision. Involve users early in the process to ensure that their input, feedback, requirements, and support is secured.

(4) **IT governance and risk**—Is the right IT infrastructure in place to support the solution being considered? Has everything possible been done to minimize IT risks, such as application integration, service levels, strategies evaluated and aligned, disaster recovery and roll-back strategies, and the like.

(5) **Success metrics and strategy**—Design a roadmap with clearly defined outcome success metrics. Weight each criterion. Are success metrics aligned with strategy?

(6) **Change process**—What type of change process will be utilized and who will administer and monitor it?

(7) **User input and requirements gathering**—Base the solution decision on the requirements of the company, users, and business issues the solution needs to solve rather than attractive but unnecessary features and functionality.

(8) **Training and development**—What training is required for system administrators and users to ensure that they are proficient in using and administering the system? Do they require any additional training to

address identified skill gaps? Has the cost of training been fully factored into the project's budget?

(9) **User adoption**—To ensure user adoption of the final system, users need to be included at the outset of the IT project. This will ensure all their requirements have been appropriately sourced, including all aspects of scoping (such as the user interface design). By involving users at the outset, they will also feel included and be more inclined to take ownership of the new system when it goes into production.

(10) **Vendor and solution selection**—Make sure that the vendors selected are the right fit because they will be with the organization for a very long time. Make sure that their solution meets business requirements rather than fitting the organization around their solution. Their solution or service offering must be their core business, with a proven track record and not a secondary business offering or service. Their solution must be inclusive of training, maintenance and support, licensing, documentation, testing, and account management, with no extra hidden costs. Also be aware that if the vendors have a hidden agenda to increase their revenue from the project by introducing ancillary add-ons or services, organizations can be certain the core project will not receive their full attention.

# Stop Blaming the Software

## Profiling the External Value Chain

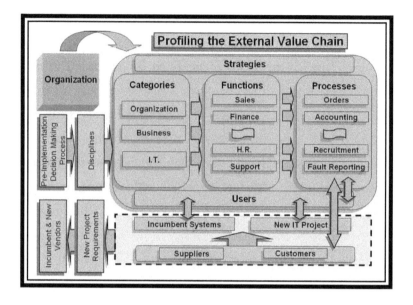

Irrespective of what strategy an organization pursues or what benefits the new IT system will deliver, the organization needs to identify how and where its customers and suppliers will either impact or be affected by the new system and processes. If an organization is pursuing a strategy to catapult it into the status of "Industry Leader," it will most certainly need a stronger alliance and tighter integration with its upstream or downstream customer processes.

By recognizing how internal and external value chain relationships impact upon their business and outcomes, elucidation of what criteria the solution needs to address based upon the performance measures an organization is aiming to address becomes more evident.

When a project impacts upon an organization's customers and suppliers, profiling the external customer value chain is one of the most important steps in identifying requirements for the ncw IT system. It is, however, a step that is easily forgotten, under-profiled, and under analyzed either by the organization or by its customers.

When profiling processes or identifying appropriate information sources it is important to ensure that they have been identified in the organization's profile. Not just because someone has said that this is the process or that these are the requirements, because invariably they are not 100% correct. Organizations need to ensure that the same rigor applied to profiling their internal organization is also applied to profiling their external value chain customers to correctly identify their requirements.

Project outcomes will not meet the expectations of either an organization or its customers if it is not as diligent in identifying its customers' requirements as rigorously as its own. Where an organization's customers' executives think they know how their entire organizations operate and what all their business and user requirements are, the risk is even greater.

## *Profiling Information for the External Value Chain*

> o Identify the organization's external upstream suppliers and downstream customers
> o Identify any common or integrated processes between them and the organization
> o Identify where and how their processes integrate with the organization's processes
> o Identify common systems and where they interface with the organization's systems

> - Do any third parties or vendors need to be involved to make process or programming changes to ensure that the new system can still process and support customers' and suppliers' transactions?
> - If yes, identify the vendor, third party, or owners of the systems or processes
> - What are the inputs or outputs? i.e. hard or electronic data, formatting, tangible items—paper forms and other data sources?
> - Will any of these inputs or outputs require changes for the new system to support them?

Profiling the organization's external value chain generates lucidity and a clear understanding of the connectedness of relationships between upstream and downstream customers, suppliers, and the organization. This allows identification of common and integrated processes or systems as well as sharing business strategies and identifying common objectives.

## The Primary Benefits of Profiling the External Value Chain

(a) **Business and user requirements** need to be sought from the external value chain as well as all internal departments affected by the proposed IT project. Profiling the internal and external value chain reduces the paucity of the projects' requirements and the IT solutions' scope by clearly highlighting all parties that need to be involved. Involving all appropriate parties also mitigates the risk of IT executives working in relative isolation. Additionally, it reduces the risk of not taking into account or omitting external value chain requirements until the system is ready to go into production, by which time it is too late.

(b) **Analysis of the external industry value chain** will also identify those vendors with a proven track record and successful partnerships within the same industry as the organization. It also identifies which vendors specialize in software solutions as their core business function rather than as a secondary business offering.

# CHAPTER

# 9

# Decision
# Making

*"Informed decision-making comes from a long tradition of
guessing and then blaming others for inadequate results"*
Scott Adams

# Decision Making

This step profiles the IT investment decision by identifying common reasons why organizations initiate IT projects, how these decisions are made, and who and what drives the decision-making process. By profiling this process, an organization can ensure that its decision making is rigorous, collaborative, and comprehensive, and that the decisions have full accountability. Decisions made before the investment and subsequent implementation will lay a solid foundation for the project.

More importantly, because these decisions are strategic to the project's success, the organization must ensure that executives making them are accountable and that their decisions are well supported. If this is not the case then the operational and tactical decisions that follow will be at risk of being unsupported and misaligned with corporate strategy or, worse, may be *adhoc* or unfounded. When executives make strategic decisions in isolation, these decisions will often not be fully supported by peers or by the organization.

Organizations tend to rely on departments or groups to make collective decisions, without specific individuals being held accountable for the quality of the final outcome. Each member of the group or department needs to be responsible for the quality of their input, but ultimately only one person can be held accountable for the overall quality of his or her group's decisions.

A much worse scenario is where an individual makes a unilateral decision on behalf of his/her group or department without consultation or input from the group or their peers but still holds the group accountable rather than themselves. By appointing a single person to be accountable for the final decision, the quality of input and analysis of the situation is more likely to be comprehensive, collaborative, and conclusive. This ensures that the final decision will be sound because it will have been made objectively based on hard facts.

## What Drives the IT Investment Decision and Why?

Our ability to understand new technologies and the business benefits they will deliver far exceeds our ability to comprehend the complex IT implementation processes required to bring an IT project to fruition. Think about it! Whether an organization is considering adopting an emergent or disruptive technology, or installing a major IT system, it will undoubtedly understand the benefits the technology will deliver but it will be quite unlikely to fully comprehend the intricate details involved in implementing them.

When implementing complex systems, organizations may believe that because they are spending a large amount of money and have committed considerable resources to the project they will have a better understanding of the complexities of the implementation. However, with emergent and disruptive innovations such as the introduction of PDAs and the massive popularity of the Palm Pilot in the mid 1990s, due to their relatively low investment costs and pervasiveness, many organizations did not realize the complexities involved in implementing a corporate-wide deployment of promising enterprise applications based on that technology. Although they understood the obvious benefits these devices could deliver as low-cost business tools, it was only a few years later, when wireless technology emerged creating the Smartphone category, that both PDA and data-enabled phone technologies were able to deliver the much sought-after business benefits. Look at what BlackBerry® is doing for corporate collaboration today.

Considering the competitive global and customer-driven environment in which organizations operate, they will be driven to constantly evolve to meet new demands. Consequently, an organization will often implement IT systems as a means to enable its evolution, increase profitability, find new ways to reduce costs, meet or exceed customer needs, and ultimately gain a competitive advantage.

With the above in mind, it is vital that an organization can clearly state the rationale and business case that supports its decision to invest in new IT systems. Some of the common reasons for investing are:

(1)   A changing business or external environment
(2)   The incumbent system is out of date and cannot handle new requirements
(3)   The vendor no longer supports the incumbent system
(4)   IT budget deadlines to spend before the end of the tax or financial year
(5)   To gain competitive advantage

(6)  An emergent or disruptive technology

(7)  Change of strategy

(8)  Increased efficiencies

(9)  Reduced operating costs

(10) To meet customer demands.

### *Profiling Information for the 'What' and 'Why' of the Decision*

> o  What external factors have driven the decision to invest in a new IT system and why?
>
> o  What internal factors have driven the decision to invest and why?
>
> o  What are the primary objectives of the system?
>
> o  What expected benefits will the system deliver to the organization, functions, and business units?
>
> o  What organizational needs will the new system address?
>
> o  Why are these needs important? Rate each need between 1-5, with 5 being the highest importance
>
> o  What is the business case supporting the project?

## Who Drives the IT Investment Decision?

Just assuming that Organization, Business, and IT will collectively drive and support the IT project investment decision is a bad oversight. This can often happen because individual, departmental, or functional objectives are misaligned with the project's objectives, or because people don't have the same vested interest in the project and its anticipated benefits. This will complicate efforts to obtain consensus. To avoid these situations, organizations need to ensure that the project's objectives link

# Decision Making

corporate, business, and IT strategies in order to achieve business performance objectives.

During the IT Investment decision-making process, the Organization, Business, and IT categories can easily become entangled and bogged down in a not-too-subtle tug of war, with each side hoping to improve its own position. This is a normal response, and identifying each entity's motivations and individual wants is critical to maintaining a common perspective during the vital strategic investment decision process. For example:

(1) IT directors look to improve or justify their IT infrastructure and system integration capabilities
(2) Finance directors look for the most economically sound solutions from a business finance perspective
(3) Business analysts look for comprehensive data analysis capabilities
(4) General managers look for a good user interface, ease of use, and business process capabilities

A collaborative approach in making a decision based on consensus is essential to ensure that the organization achieves optimal Organization, Business, and IT-based input that will collectively drive and support the decision.

Often it is the 'What' driving the IT investment decision that will determine 'Who' is driving the decision process. For example, an HR and Payroll implementation will most likely be driven by the HR Director. Irrespective of Who and What, the decision should still be tied back to the organization's strategy and bottom-line benefits to ensure full organizational support and to improve the chances of the project's success.

# Stop Blaming the Software

Depending on the size of an organization, either the CEO or Board of Directors will set the organization's goals and direction. The CEO will then implement strategic plans to achieve these goals by liaising between the Business and IT functions and building a vision to ensure all entities have a clear understanding of the organization's chosen direction. In collaboration, they will then determine business unit strategies to ensure that they are aligned and support the organization in achieving its overall strategic goals.

The CIO will determine the technology strategy to support the overall organization and business strategy, and will also determine whether the incumbent hardware and IT infrastructure is capable of supporting the new system or what additional IT infrastructure is required.

If the organization does not fully fund the investment, the CFO and/or COO will set the budget and business unit's contributions to the investment according to their usage.

## *Profiling Information for the 'Who' of the Decision*

- o Who is the project sponsor? (The person in the organization who proposed the IT system and will be accountable for it until the project's conclusion.)
- o Who in the organization made the IT investment decision?
- o Who is driving the decision to invest?
- o Is the Project Sponsor also the decision driver?
- o If this is not the same person, what are the specific reasons for that person being the Project Sponsor?

# Decision Making

> o   Do all of the relevant senior executives support the investment decision? (Note that even indirectly affected executives need to be included in answering this question.)
> o   What are their reasons for agreeing with and supporting the investment decision?
> o   What reasons were given for disagreeing with the decision?

## How was the IT Investment Decision Made?

If Organization, Business, and IT are collectively driving the decision to invest in a new IT system, was the decision made collaboratively with input secured from all C-Level and senior executives, managers, stakeholders, and all affected departments?

Often, IT investment decisions are made according to one or a combination of the following criteria:

- The decision is made collectively based upon everyone's input
- Everyone agrees with the decision but no one is held accountable for the supporting evidence and business case
- The decision is deferred to a person in authority, or someone who has expertise or some other form of power that edifies them and their decision so that they or their decisions are uncontested
- The decision is made with little or no input from relevant people and departments that will be impacted
- The decision is made in isolation by just one or two executives
- The decision is made at the club between friends or colleagues

# Stop Blaming the Software

Unless an organization has a stringent decision-making process, strategic decisions can often be made in isolation with little input or consultation from the appropriate people, groups, or departments that need to be involved. This may sound foreign to some organizations but to others it will sound all too familiar.

However, even where organizations outwardly appear to apply rigor to their IT decisions, closer inspection will often reveal that their decision-making process may be biased and have flawed attributes that are not so obvious to unsuspecting parties. This may sound harsh or unrealistic, but a careful analysis of your organization's last IT investment decision, how it was made, and by whom, could reveal subtle biases in contributions.

Organizations also need to be aware that even though the initial decision to invest in a new IT system is made at executive level, it is the business and users that need to be involved before requesting vendor proposals. If those who should be involved have no say in the IT decision or project requirements, the decision will be based on incomplete and inaccurate information.

Additionally, if people feel they or their input have been excluded from the decision-making process, they will assume they were dismissed as irrelevant, which will foster resentment and passive aggressive behavior. This, in turn, will often result in a decision that is not fully supported, one which will be made in spite of those who should have been consulted, not because of them.

The impact of informal communications networks that often extend beyond an organization also needs to be identified and considered. Based on the eclectic input from these networks organizations will often be able to improve the quality of their decisions. The people in these networks are linked to customers and suppliers both upstream and downstream of the organization and are generally at the organization's coal face or at a grassroots level within it. They often have solid relationships and communications with customers and suppliers. Consequently, both parties informally discuss and share incidental information, such current events in their organization, their jobs, and current issues. These people can often provide relevant information and input into requirements for a new IT system, which, from a strategic level, may not have been identified. Leaving these people and their communication networks untapped could impact on the success of the project either by not gaining their support or by fostering a passive aggressive attitude.

## *Profiling Information for the 'How' of a Decision*

- o Based upon Who made the IT investment decision, How was the decision actually made? Collectively, collaboratively, or in isolation?
- o Who was involved in the investment decision-making process and How were they involved?
- o What input from the relevant C-level personnel, senior executives, and managers supports and evidences the above answer?
- o How did they quantify their reasons and support for the investment decision?
- o Have all appropriate internal users and stakeholders been included in the investment decision? How have they been involved?
- o What external parties have been included in the investment decision and How have they been involved?

# CHAPTER

# 10

# IT Risk
# and
# Governance

*"Government does not solve problems; it subsidizes them"*
Ronald Reagan

# IT Risk and Governance

IT risk and governance is an extensive, multi-faceted process or framework around which organizations link IT and business strategies. It ensures that due process achieves the desired organizational goals and objectives and that appropriate success metrics are applied to ensure IT projects achieve their stated business objectives.

## Minimizing IT Risk

The extent to which IT governance measures are required to satisfy the desired outcomes for stakeholders depends largely on the organization's size, its industry, and regulations.

Risk is inherent in any IT project and an organization needs to take this into account before initiating a project. More important are the plans made to identify and mitigate these risks before implementing them and what processes are established to manage and minimize risk during the project.

A vital step in minimizing IT risk is to establish an IT governance framework. This is a key element in understanding and controlling the use of IT in an organization by ensuring that all parties involved in the IT decision-making process have a common understanding of how risks will be dealt with and minimized particularly for new technology projects. It will also ensure that corporate, business, and IT strategies are aligned. A comprehensive IT governance framework will encompass all aspects of IT that need to be addressed when an organization is considering undertaking an IT implementation. Each aspect poses different possible risks to a project.

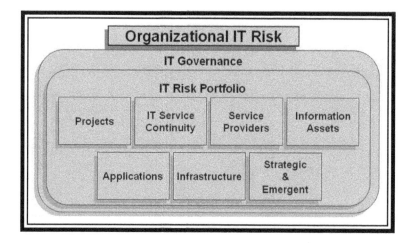

Source: Adapted from Jordan, E Silcock, L 2005, 'Beating IT risk,' John Wiley & Sons Ltd, West-Sussex England.

a.  IT governance ensures that sufficient financial and human resources are available to support the implementation, ongoing use, and maintenance throughout the life of the system.

b.  An IT risk portfolio approach enables a comprehensive understanding of the integration between services, applications, infrastructure, management, the business benefits, and strategic alignment.

# IT Risk and Governance

The IT portfolio pulls together all IT risks under one umbrella to ensure that completeness, connectedness, and the significance of all IT risk areas are recognized and monitored concurrently. An organization using an IT risk portfolio approach will thereby minimize the risk of IT mismatches by addressing matters such as:

(1) Reducing the chance of investing in applications or systems that cannot be supported by current infrastructure.

(2) Creating awareness of incumbent service providers or vendors and regularly monitoring their adherence to Service Level Agreements (SLAs). The level of attention given to the organization, its level of accountability when things go wrong, and any changes in its core business.

(3) Ensuring that the application or solution works to specification, that it is scalable, capable of integration, flexible and functional, and that appropriate user involvement takes place to ensure the system is designed to achieve its stated purpose for the organization and its end users.

(4) Creating visibility of new and emergent technologies in order to avoid obsolescence. Without this visibility, IT implementations may risk being superseded by new technologies even before the current implementation is completed.

In addition to monitoring IT risk, an organization should also conduct a rigorous pre-investment Risk Profile and Risk Assessment on projects. Using a risk assessment approach such as a weighted scorecard for new projects, including assessing any changes to existing production systems, these risk factors should be scored as to their potential failure and weighted against the ease of rollback. The scorecard should be a template that includes all the usual factors and a pre-agreed weighting for each factor. Multiple parties can then score the factors, results can be aggregated, and the average and/or median taken to create a combined risk assessment. This will help identify foreseeable obstacles and uncover more subtle and less obvious risks that may negatively impact the implementation process. This Risk Profile will also highlight deficiencies that may exist concerning the organization's level of technical expertise, project management, and leadership.

By providing complete transparency into the capabilities and deficiencies in these areas, IT risks that could negatively impact a company's strategic initiatives will be clearly identified before the project starts. They can then be mitigated or eliminated before they create problems.

## Profiling IT Risk and Governance

IT risk and governance measures need to be rigorously applied so they are permanently imbued in the organization's culture, thereby making IT risk management a formal day-to-day function, rather than an *adhoc* occurrence. Whether the IT project is a major implementation or a minor upgrade, an IT risk framework will create and ensure consistency in procedures between current and future IT projects. To ensure that future projects have the best chance of succeeding, these same procedures must therefore be carried forward.

At the very minimum, an organization needs to build an IT checklist for any project, big or small. Consider the checklists pilots use before takeoff and landing. Yes, they are well trained and practice often enough to fly 999 times out of a 1,000 without needing their checklists, but would you want to be on the plane the day they missed a step or got the steps out of order?

Today's current data becomes tomorrow's useful historical data on which an organization needs to base subsequent upgrades and new IT projects. Without standardizing procedures and capturing information and data pertaining to current implementations, valuable data and lessons are lost because no one will be able to accurately recall the information needed to guide future projects.

### *Profiling Information for IT Risk and Governance*

> - Has the organization ever undertaken an IT project of this complexity? If no, identify the most complex IT project undertaken?
> - Was it successful or problematic? Describe the results of either outcome
> - Does the organization have access to historical project information or processes from its previous IT projects?
> - Will any of this data be useful for this IT project, and how relevant is it?
> - Does the organization have an IT governance framework that is rigorously used?
> - Does the organization have an IT governance framework that is rarely applied to IT projects?
> - Do senior executives fully comprehend the level of project complexity and organizational change this project will entail? How or what actions have they taken to show comprehension and commitment?

o Does the IT department have the level of technical expertise required for this IT project?

o Will the IT department rely heavily on a third party vendor, developer, or systems implementer's skills and expertise?

o If the IT department plans to rely on a third party, what skills, expertise, or knowledge, in particular, does it require from the third party?

o Are these skills that would prove beneficial for the organization to invest in its employees?

o Does the Project Sponsor have the necessary leadership skills to guide the project to completion? Or will the Project Sponsor inadvertently relinquish control to a third party when the going gets tough or if the project is extended?

o What other projects has the Project Sponsor successfully led prior to this project?

o Does the Project Sponsor need to be overseen or trained?

## Organizations with IT Governance but Failed IT Projects

It is surprising to find that many large organizations and government bodies that claim to have stringent IT Governance frameworks still have rogue, runaway, or failed IT projects. The following are just a few examples of such organizations and references to their rogue projects:

- **The USA Census Bureau**

  $2 billion in IT project overruns for a project that will probably need to be scrapped!

  http://blogs.zdnet.com/projectfailures/?p=660&tag=nl.e539

- **Avis Car Rental—Europe ERP Project**

  €45 million IT failure as ERP Project is cancelled.

  http://www.zdnet.com.au/news/business/soa/Avis-bins-PeopleSoft-system-after-45m-IT—failure/0,139023166,139164049,00.htm

- **Melbourne Transportation Authority Australia—Myki project**

  $1billion later and 18 months behind schedule delivering Project "Myki"

  http://www.australianit.news.com.au/story/0,24897,23155542-15319,00.html

- **Australian Ports—Integrated Cargo System**

  $217 billion cost blowout for a system that still does not work as it was intended to.

  http://www.australianit.news.com.au/story/0,24897,17011260-15317,00.html

- **FBI—VCF project**

  $170 million for an IT project that had to be cancelled

  http://www.washingtonpost.com/wp-dyn/content/article/2006/08/17/AR2006081701485_pf.html

- **Sydney Water—CIBS project**

  Estimated $97 million blowout and lengthy delays for a project that was scrapped

  http://blogs.zdnet.com/projectfailures/?p=506

# Stop Blaming the Software

If you go to these links and read the abovementioned reports, you will get the impression that these organizations and vendors are blameless for their obvious failures. All of them claim that, at the time they entered into the project, they believed the other party had the level of expertise, skills, and knowledge to fully understand the complexity of the project and what was being requested. As explained in earlier chapters, these poor assumptions were made at the pre-implementation phase and the root cause of these failures was that key project decisions received insufficient attention or were completely overlooked.

If these organizations had undertaken corporate profiling and heeded their findings, they would have had visibility into their project and the organization's requirements at the pre-implementation stage. This would have enabled a clearer decision-making process, thereby avoiding or minimizing these disasters.

An extract on the Sydney Water project failure highlights the defensive posture of the "not so innocent" scapegoats in question.

> *"I was surprised at the extent to which responses from both Sydney Water and PwC relied on plausible deniability, nitpicking, and hair-splitting to avoid responsibility. PwC basically denied the failure altogether".*

Reference: Michael Krigsman,
http://blogs.zdnet.com/projectfailures/?p=506, December 1st 2007

What these organizations all effectively achieved during their post-implementation reviews was to find scapegoats for each aspect of non-delivery and budget overruns. Their vendors took the brunt of their attacks, which comes as no surprise because no organization wants to be held accountable to its stakeholders for failures of that magnitude.

Vendors implementing packaged solutions, bespoke developments, consulting or project managing the implementation all failed. The question is why?

Ask yourself, how so many established vendors could be so incompetent in their areas of expertise? And why are there so many software packages that are so useless? The answers—the vendors are not incompetent and the software packages are not useless. QED. The problems all stem from a lack of corporate profiling practices.

## What Constitutes an Implementation Failure and Who Determines the Success of a Project?

Depending on who within an organization is asked whether an IT implementation was successful or not, responses will differ.

Possibly because the CIO provides technical recommendations for the system, and project managers are tasked with implementing the system, they do not want to appear to have failed and will claim the project to be a "technical success" (they won the battle but the organization lost the war). This just confuses what constitutes a successful implementation and what does not.

IT professionals and C-level executives can often confuse an IT system that is "successfully implemented to specification" with implementing a functional system that delivers agreed business benefits and is used effectively by the organization for the purpose for which it was intended. In other words, the implementation was a technical success but the benefits the company expected to receive in terms of generating growth, increased efficiencies, or achieving bottom-line savings were not realized.

When the Project Manager, IT Manager, or CIO considers an IT implementation to be a success this isn't necessarily the opinion of the users. An IT implementation that is a "technical success" may be a failure in the eyes of the customer and the organization if it underperforms or is under-adopted by the users. Where users are also the customers or stakeholders, their opinions are the ultimate measure of an IT project's success.

Independent definitions of "failed implementations" vary depending upon the title and position of the person providing the definition. Not all IT project failures necessarily constitute a major time or budget blowout, but this type of implementation failure cannot be misconstrued and doesn't require further "interpretation" of the facts.

Nevertheless, when Sydney Water's IT implementation went over budget by more than $80 million its response was to euthanize the project. Even so, the vendor did not consider it a failed project but a "cancelled project" because at the time of cancellation the project was on track for delivery (totally ignoring the matter of the budget blow-out).

# IT Risk and Governance

## *Profiling Information for Interpreting the Project Outcomes*

- o Who will decide if the project implementation constitutes a success at completion?
- o How will this decision be made?
- o Will the decision be based on agreed success metrics or some other metric? If another metric, what will it be?
- o To what extent has user satisfaction and adoption of the system been factored in to determining the project's ultimate success?

# CHAPTER

# 11

# Strategy and
# Success Metrics

*"However beautiful the strategy, you should occasionally look
at the results"*
Winston Churchill

# Strategy and Success Metrics

The organization's strategy will determine what success metrics should be applied to measure the outcomes of its IT implementation. Therefore, for the organization to choose appropriate success metrics, the metrics should be applicable to measuring success against any of the four performance criteria relevant to the organization's strategy and objectives such as:

(1) Business operations
(2) Customer expectations
(3) Financial performance
(4) Company learning and improvement.

## Aligning Success Measures with Corporate Strategy

Identifying what success measures will be applied to assess the implementation's outcome will be determined by the strategy driving the organization's operations and will depend on the nature of the organization i.e. whether the organization delivers services or products.

# Stop Blaming the Software

Michael Porter, a leading strategist, recommends three generic strategies and purports that organizations need to define their strategy as either:

(a) Differentiation
(b) Cost Leadership
(c) Focus or Niche.

Porter argues that unless an organization chooses one over the others, it risks becoming stuck in the middle, and consequently neither strategy will be fully realized. However, due to the dynamic and turbulent environment in which businesses now operate, strategy is not as cut and dried as it once was. Variations of Michael Porter's generic strategies have evolved, with new strategies being developed to keep pace with an ever-changing environment.

Increasingly turbulent markets and industries, emergent market niches, competition, consumer sophistications, environmental concerns, and social responsibilities have driven organizations to adopt multipronged strategies, making them fiercer than ever. For example, in previous decades, manufacturing organizations tended to pursue a single operational excellence strategy. However, in today's demanding environment this simply isn't sufficient to remain competitive or to stay in business. Consequently, the strategies of organizations have evolved to contain an element of product leadership through innovation, some level of customer intimacy, and ensuring their manufacturing processes address increasing global environmental concerns and social responsibility issues. A multipronged strategy "can work," provided the organization's leaders fully comprehend the strategic approach and have clearly articulated these strategies to their entire organization.

Some organizations "unintentionally" adopt multipronged strategies. This is usually the case where they have a poorly or loosely defined strategy and try to please all the people all the time. Subsequently, when undertaking an IT project, they do not or cannot conclusively identify and communicate what objectives need to be achieved. Therefore, they cannot clearly define what success metrics are to be applied to measure the implementation's success.

Apply this simple test: If an organization's leaders cannot clearly articulate in 40 words or less what the organization's strategy is, then it is a safe bet that the rest of the organization doesn't understand it either.

The risk is that an unclearly articulated strategy can cause senior executives to chase disparate objectives they believe are linked to the organization's strategy. However, often these objectives are based upon their interpretation of what they understand the organization's strategy to be. Departments and employees then commit huge amounts of time and resources undertaking corporate initiatives that end up being euthanized because they don't align with another department's perception of the organization's strategic objectives. Unless the corporate strategy is clearly defined, inappropriate success metrics will also be identified.

As much as an organization's strategy and objectives need to be clearly understood and articulated, so too do the success metrics that are applied to the IT implementation. Unless those involved in the IT implementation are fully aware of what performance measures and success metrics the organization will use to measure project results and achievements, the measures will be of limited value.

To successfully drive, integrate, and sustain IT change, it is therefore imperative to ensure that the organization's core strategies are communicated to, and understood by, all business departments (including IT). This will ensure that organizational and divisional strategies and goals are aligned and underpinned by common goals. These strategies need to be supported by the relevant processes that are driven by management, supported by business, and adopted by users.

## Profiling Information for an Organization's Strategy

> o Is the corporate strategy multi-faceted? If so, clearly identify all facets.
>
> o Is the new IT system enabling a change to existing corporate strategy?
>
> o If yes, what is the change in strategy and what benefits does the organization expect to realize from it?
>
> o How will the new IT project support the new or current strategy?
>
> o What are the common objectives between the organization's strategy and the IT project?
>
> o Does the IT strategy support corporate and business strategies?

## Deciding on Success Metrics

A project's success cannot be measured without first identifying what the primary target or objectives are. Before executing an IT investment decision an organization needs to decide on the metrics that the success of the IT project will be measured against. Without an agreed pre-determined set of project success measures, evaluation of the quality and success of the IT system will be futile. This is a critical issue for all IT implementations because to be able to assess the success of a project the organization needs to know before the project commences what return it expects from its investment.

Whether success metrics are based on measuring increased efficiencies such as customer satisfaction, increased sales, reduced operational costs, or the company's ROI, the end results need to be able to be objectively quantified. In the absence of any formal predetermined metrics and clearly articulated objectives, or if it was simply assumed that certain benefits would be delivered, it is likely additional unplanned investments will be called for to achieve these benefits. The end result of this is more time and money invested, leading to the same result—an overpriced, under-delivered and under-performing IT system.

This situation comes about in many ways but a typical example is where, at some point, the Project Manager recognizes that scope-creep and new or emerging requireme4nts are creating a runaway project. At this point, the manager calls for the specification to be frozen with no more changes permitted until phase 2 (phase 1 being the first production release). Phase 1 will consume (and probably exceed) the original budget but will still not have delivered all the expected outcomes. Phase 2 and beyond promises to deliver the balance of the project, including the newly identified requirements. However, by then, the organization is committed to operating without the important unforeseen, but necessary, functionality.

## Stop Blaming the Software

This often happens when the project scope is too large or overambitious in the first place. By looking at the project budget and project timeline, it is almost certainly guaranteed that where there are massive budgets and long implementation time-frames the project will be doomed at the outset unless it can be broken into smaller phases. Be warned that it is difficult to convince organizations of this if they believe a big budget is naturally synonymous with a big delivery time frame. They may feel that to get value for money, the project size and budget need to be large scale and the time frames substantial because otherwise they will be short-changed. The two fundamental rules of thumb that influence the success of an IT implementation are to either:

(a) Spend a lot of money over a short time frame or
(b) Spend small amounts of money incrementally over an extended time frame

Either way, if an organization does not have a clearly articulated IT strategy and it does not curtail the scope of its project (according to either one of the above methods), the implementation will be at risk of failure.

It is vital success metrics are clearly articulated to all relevant people and parties involved in the project to ensure they fully understand what the organization expects and how success will be measured.

It is equally important that progress evaluation measures are established to continuously monitor the project's progress and to be alerted to the telltale signs of it becoming a runaway project. These measures may be in terms of budget, time, or achievement of agreed milestone objectives.

# Strategy and Success Metrics

## *Profiling Information for Progress and Success Metrics*

- What success metrics will the organization apply to the project's outcome? Be specific and rate them in terms of importance
- Who selected the project success metrics? What decision makers or parties specifically were involved with agreeing or disagreeing with the proposed metrics?
- Are the success metrics aligned with corporate strategy? Explain the reasons for the choice of metrics and how they are aligned to corporate strategy
- How will each success metric applied be measured?
- Who has been appointed to interpret and measure the success metrics and project outcomes?
- What project progress measures will be applied to the project and at what points or milestones? Be specific and rate them in terms of importance
- How will these be measured?
- Who has been appointed to measure them at milestones during the project's lifecycle?
- Who from the organization has been granted authority and accountability to make ongoing project decisions to remedy emerging project issues or increased costs?
- Does this person have the support of the organization?

# Stop Blaming the Software

## The Go/No-Go Decision—Euthanizing a Rogue Project

Without a Go/No-Go IT risk strategy linked to performance and progress measurements, an organization will not have an objective measure to determine when the project is on track or if it is at risk of becoming a rogue or runaway project. If the project goes into overrun mode or if the system is implemented without delivering the expected benefits and outcomes, it becomes increasingly difficult to be able to make the tricky decision on when to rein it in.

If the point at which the implementation reaches a 'no-go' decision has not been defined and agreed upon, or if the appropriate person accountable for executing the order to euthanize has not been appointed prior to the project's commencement, the decision to euthanize a project midimplementation can become so emotionally charged that no one will be willing to make the decision, let alone execute the order. It is therefore imperative a "Project Euthanizer" is appointed and has established up front the point at which a project overrun becomes unacceptable.

Appointing a suitable Project Euthanizer to a project is a major decision and one that needs to be carefully thought through before the project commences. Often, because the CIO or IT Executive are personally involved in an IT project that has already been heavily invested in, they may be unwilling to euthanize it. Similarly, the Project Sponsor is likely to be emotionally attached to the project and will not be inclined to make the tough call to pull the plug. Consequently, the organization needs to appoint a senior person who will be in a position of objectivity and who will be able to take the pressure that comes with executing such a decision.

Different people will also have differing views of what is an acceptable project overrun. Therefore, organizations need to decide on these parameters at the outset and be prepared to take action for specific legitimate reasons to renegotiate the parameters. If the decision to euthanize the project is made, be prepared to hear the arguments "we are nearly finished" or "there are no more than six weeks to go." But bear in mind the "mythical" last 10% of projects often takes 50% plus of the total time.

## *Profiling Information for Making the Go/No-Go Decision*

---

o Who has been appointed Project Euthanizer responsible and accountable for executing the Go/No-Go decision? Does she or he have the total support of the organization and relevant third parties?

o Does he/she need to consult with any other parties before executing this decision? If so, please name the specific parties to be consulted

o Who will determine if and when the project has become a runaway?

o Is this the same person as the Project Euthanizer? If so, what are the reasons, and how and who will ensure that objectivity is maintained?

o What criteria will be used to decide whether the project is rogue or has become a runaway?

o What time frame over the projected duration is acceptable and unacceptable?

---

- o How much over budget is acceptable and unacceptable?
- o If using other criteria, please be explicit and define exactly what other reasons or measures will be used to determine a Go/No-Go decision
- o If people raise objections about terminating the project, who and how will these objections be dealt with?
- o Who and how will these objections be assessed for relevance?

# CHAPER

# 12

# Communications and Requirements Gathering

*"Start with good people, lay out the rules, communicate with your employees, motivate them and reward them. If you do all those things effectively, you can't miss"*

Lee Iacocca

# Communications and Requirements Gathering

A common misconception about IT project failures is that they are primarily due to IT mismanagement, poor hardware and software selection, or poor project—management skills. This is seldom the case. With very few exceptions, the major cause of IT project failures is attributable to a lack of effective communications between senior executives, IT, and the rest of the organization. This is evidenced by poor user requirements, inaccurate or unarticulated project information, and a lack of support at the very outset of the project. Often poor communications processes and incomplete or inaccurate project requirements can be traced back to the initial pre-IT investment decision-making and pre-implementation planning process itself.

Even though the IT Department and Project Managers are excellent at overseeing project implementations, they can only work with the requirements and directives agreed upon and communicated to them. Therefore, effective and appropriate communication channels must be established before a project starts so they receive accurate and complete information with which to manage the project.

## Stop Blaming the Software

Profiling the organization's communication channels and information sources will enable it to identify and effectively communicate project information and expected outcomes to the appropriate people, departments, and third parties. It will also help identify why and where in the organization communication channels need to be established and from where and from whom to source project, business, and user requirements.

At the project's outset it is vital end users are identified so their requirements can be taken into account in the scoping, analysis, and design phases of the project. Their inclusion in the communications process at this early stage will ensure they appreciate and understand that their input is important and that they are responsible for ensuring their input is accurate and complete.

If correct communication channels and sources are not identified at the outset, requirements cannot be expected to be accurate or extensive enough to correctly specify or scope the project.

### Corporate communications

Effective communications are most commonly achieved by face-to-face meetings. Whether they are one-on-one discussions, group meetings, or video conferences, they will promote open and honest communications at all levels. Such verbal communications enable people to deliver and exchange information, be understood, and discuss project matters interactively for clarification. A follow-up email, minutes, or memos recording points of the meeting provide ongoing reminders that need no further interpretation.

With the proliferation of communication-enabling technologies such as online discussion forums, email, instant messaging, SMS, social networking, blogs, and the like, a great deal of informal information tends to fly around. As useful as they are, none of these mediums can ever substitute for, or be as effective as, face-to-face communications, followed up with a written record of what was discussed and agreed. These technologies have their place in an organization but should not feature too prominently or dominate communication methods for an IT project. These technologies cannot always be relied on to ensure the message has been correctly received, understood, and interpreted.

To ensure the organization is well prepared for its proposed IT implementation, it must ensure effective, open, honest, and multidirectional communications takes place between the critical components that have causal interconnected relationships with the respective parties. Because an IT implementation relies on shared information and ideas and is driven by aligned strategies and objectives, comprehensive multidirectional communications are essential to achieving a successful outcome. Keep in mind though, that even if an organization claims to have an "open-door policy," it may not necessarily be open to hearing ideas or input until things start going askew. That is when they wonder what went wrong and why this hadn't been brought to their attention earlier. It was, but they were inattentive and didn't take the ideas and suggestions of others seriously. This is called the "open-door closed-mind" policy. Ensure that closed minds aren't prevalent in the organization when undertaking an IT project.

Without comprehensively profiling all corporate communications channels, the organization will not fully recognize where most of the required information and data needs to come from. It then becomes highly probable that critical project information will be hidden because key informal or indirect sources of information that can contribute a wealth of input to the project are not identified. Ask yourself when last you discovered all too late that missing information from a channel that had not been considered as an information source caused an issue with a project.

Corporate communications channels are critical in situations where the organization needs to formally communicate information. These channels are equally critical when undertaking an IT implementation. During this period of change and turmoil, the organization needs to ensure it has a clearly defined communications strategy based upon its corporate profile. This will identify the communication direction, sources, and channels between all parties involved, as well as establish a method for giving and receiving feedback. This will greatly facilitate addressing critical implementation failure factors caused by incomplete, ineffective, and poor communications.

A communications strategy must include upward, downward, and cross-communications throughout the entire organization rather than just between IT and senior executives. All communications must not just address the "What, When, Who, and How" from one person's perspective. Who communicates What, When, How, and to Whom should be from a corporate-wide perspective to ensure a collaborative decision is made. More than one person delivering the same information can often cause confusion such as, "I thought he/she said" or "we were told something different to what the other department were told."

These communications must articulate the organization's needs, what the user's requirements are, the purpose of the investment, what the expected benefits and outcomes

# Communications and Requirements Gathering

arc, how the project will progress, and how its success will be measured. Additionally, communications need to be undertaken with all departments, users, upstream and downstream suppliers and customers who have been identified as either affecting or being impacted by the new IT system so they understand and can be prepared for the upcoming changes.

## The six key features integral to a communications strategy should include

(a) Directionality—top down and bottom up communications
(b) Role—the nature of what is being communicated from whom to whom
(c) Source—the integrity of communications sources, their quality, reliability, and appropriateness
(d) Content integration—internal and external information
(e) Channel—how will the information be communicated and will such communication distort or dilute its meaning
(f) Feedback—how and who will receive and interpret feedback in a timely manner

A good communications strategy will ensure the organization's objectives, and its important success measures are clearly communicated to those involved in the implementation. It will also ensure they are all fully aware of what is to be measured and what the quantifiable outcomes are so they understand what the organization expects to achieve. Everyone must pursue common goals, otherwise corporate objectives and success measures will be undermined.

# Stop Blaming the Software

## *Profiling Information for an Organization's Communications*

To begin profiling an organization's communications the key project decision makers need to be identified. Most of these people will have been identified in the chapter on "Decision-making."

Firstly, identify the following top-level people and parties involved in the IT project decision. One or occasionally more than one of these people must be the primary source of project-specific communications to the organization and other relevant parties. Further on in this chapter we will identify the recipients of these communications who need to be included in the overall communications process since they will be the sources for relevant project information and requirements.

Specifically name each top-level person involved:

- Project Sponsor
- IT investment decision makers
- IT department contacts
- Project Managers (internal and or external)
- C-Level executives
- Senior executives supporting the investment decision
- Managers
- Stakeholders supporting the investment decision

Due to the nature of these people's role in a project, they need to be able to collaborate and communicate with each other to ensure they are all 100% committed to the organization's common objectives. If there is a lack of sideways (peer-level) communications and collaboration between these parties, support for the project will wane. Where people feel isolated or are excluded from the project's decisions, they will turn their attention elsewhere and their support will be lost.

Senior executives must provide cohesive top-down communications, stating objectives and reasons for undertaking the IT project, what the benefits to the organization will be, how it will impact the organization, its people and other aspects such as time frames and milestones. They must also have processes in place for receiving and effectively responding to feedback and queries.

This initial communication to the organization about the project needs to be done formally rather than people hearing it through the corporate grapevine. Even though we all dread hearing bad news, if a project involves a corporate restructure or downsizing, it is best "where possible" to inform people in advance. If people become suspicious of the organization's intentions, not only will their support for the project be lost but TVC (thinly veiled contempt) will likely emerge and spread rapidly through the organization. Communications will ensure the entire organization is prepared and knows what to expect from the project.

These initial primary communications are pivotal because they will indicate to the rest of the organization whether management views them as important or inconsequential to the organization's being. So, it is these initial communications that set the stage for determining how "seamlessly" or not the organization will adopt the change and support the project.

A lack of understanding and communications between IT and business is also a major factor that contributes to IT failures. Some years ago, I witnessed such a case at a major Roads Authority in Australia.

# Stop Blaming the Software

My company collaborated with a Business Unit of the Roads Authority and had developed several systems for efficiently reporting on bridge and road maintenance, work scheduling, and cost estimations. These systems allowed workers to use hand-held computers to gather information during the day. This information was then synchronized with a central database.

Following a successful deployment of about two years, the Business Unit asked for the system to be expanded, at which point their IT department became involved. Rather than staying with their existing system, they decided to put the project out to tender to obtain the best possible proposal. What their IT department failed to understand was how the business was already realizing benefits and costs savings from their existing system that had already been deployed. The successful vendor (not my company) naively agreed to unrealistic performance hurdles that were not only unattainable but were linked to project progress payments. When these progress payments were withheld (in keeping with their contract), the vendor eventually ended up going out of business and the system was never delivered.

This is a classic lose-lose scenario because IT did not fully understand what the business actually needed.

## *Profiling Information for Internal Communications and Requirement Sources*

Having profiled the organization's top-level decision makers and primary sources for project communications, the second task is to identify the recipients of these communications.

These people and parties are the important internal communication and information sources for a project. They need to communicate back to the organization their business and user requirements, be solicited for input and feedback, and identify the needs and wants of end users.

Specifically name the following parties:

o Functions, business units, or departments (these have already been delineated through the organization's profile)

o Executives or managers of these functions or departments

o Users from these functions or departments

o Internal users of the incumbent system

o Intended internal users of the new system

Unless a system is stand-alone or a "point solution," most functions or departments within the organization will either directly or indirectly have access to the incumbent or new system. By profiling all departments, functions, executives, and users, it can be easily identified where, how, and if any of these parties will be impacted by the change. Obviously, those functions or departments that do not or will not interface or have no contact with the incumbent or new system can be ignored. However, the entire organization should stay informed on the progress of the project.

The departments, functions, executives, and users that will be impacted by the change need to be identified for specific communications in order to obtain their input. Project communications at this level need to be top-down and bottom-up, with an effective formal mechanism in place to give, receive, and manage feedback and also to solicit input. These communications need to be conducted formally and verbally (with written records of these meetings) to ensure messages are received correctly and fully understood. It is also an opportunity for responding to legitimate questions, informal sharing of information, building rapport and providing support.

Keep in mind that it is often the prolific informal sideways communications within a business that will either benefit or hinder a project. These communications can also be a rich source of informal information, new ideas, and grassroots customer information that may not always be shared upwards because such feedback and input is not always solicited, encouraged, or acted upon.

An example I came across recently involved a customer service officer and his customer who were sorting out a consignment problem over the phone. Both mentioned how busy they were and the service officer described a new system that was going live in the next six months and how much easier it would make his job. The customer discussed how it could impact on his work since both organizations, and especially his job function, would need to interface with the new system. He considered mentioning it to his management but on previous occasions when operational changes had been made the management had neglected to communicate these changes to him. Therefore, he incorrectly assumed management was already aware of the new system their supplier was implementing. He knew from experience that only senior-level staff within his organization were allowed to communicate with management. Consequently, the new IT system went into production without either organization liaising on the all-important operational changes. This fallout cost both organizations a substantial loss of business and revenue—all of which could have been avoided had feedback mechanisms encouraging employee input been implemented.

This is the reason why an organization must establish clear, honest, and open communications with its employees, encouraging their input and feedback. Users at the grassroots level of an organization are often closer to its customers than is assumed.

## *Profiling Information for External Value Chain Requirements*

Finally, the organization's external customers and suppliers need to be identified. These external parties need to be profiled for user and project requirements and also be included in project communications because they could impact the outcome of a project in terms of requirements or support.

Specifically name the following parties:

> o External upstream suppliers
> o Senior executive contacts of upstream suppliers' organizations
> o Upstream suppliers' users of the incumbent system (people who input or extract information from the system)
> o Intended upstream suppliers' users of the new system
> o External downstream customers
> o Senior executive contacts of downstream customers' organizations
> o Downstream customers' users of the incumbent system
> o Intended downstream customers' users of the new system

Depending upon whether an organization provides services or products will determine the extent of its external value chain. Not every customer or supplier will interface with the organization's IT systems, but very often any type of communications with them or exchanging data in any form, will require some level of integration. Therefore, identifying all customers and suppliers at the outset will determine who to communicate with about the proposed IT implementation.

This will also help the parties involved to recognize where the system will interface with other systems and what requirements need to be identified in the project scoping and planning phases. Often, when there's a rush to identify organizational requirements for the IT system, organizations can forget to fully identify its external suppliers and customers and the project's potential impact on their operations.

For example, a minor change such as altering the paper color of a ticket can have serious ramifications. This actually happened some time ago in Australia when a national bank decided to automate its manual credit card transaction data entry system for paper tickets (or vouchers) that were created by card imprinters (when they were still in popular use). Their aim was to reduce the labor costs involved in rekeying transaction data from these paper credit card transaction records into their system. Their tests on the new system used only common white paper tickets and projected that the average reject rate (where the system read the data incorrectly) would be around five percent. No one checked with one of their largest customers, a massive national department chain that used "blue" credit card transaction paper not white. When the system went live, 70% of the transaction tickets were rejected because, although humans could read black ink on blue paper, the system could not.

This resulted in a massive disaster where credit card transactions could not be processed for months and were stacked floor to ceiling in boxes. The simple issue of paper color could have been avoided if the bank had communicated with all of their major customers and had gathered representative samples/

requirements. Had they asked their own employees who actually performed the manual data entry work they would also have been alerted to the paper color issue. But they were just "lowly" data entry operators who were excluded from any of the discussions.

Once an organization has profiled its communications sources, the where, how, and with whom the critical communications take place becomes evident. These communication sources also become starting points and sources for requirements gathering.

## External Value Chain Communications

To ensure that communications with the external value chain are effective, the organization needs to identify and appoint the primary contact for technical and business communications between the organization and its upstream suppliers and downstream customers. It is essential the appointee communicates implementation progress updates and issues to customers and suppliers that are involved in the implementation. These customers and suppliers will have been identified through the organization and communications profile, and they will also be good sources of input into the project requirements. This is why establishing correct communications with the appropriately identified parties at the project's outset is important not only for good all-round communications but also for input, support, and requirements gathering.

By involving customers, suppliers, and stakeholders in discussions regarding their requirements and communicating with them on planned changes, they will remain informed on what impact the changes will have on them. The organization's profile will highlight where and how the organization and its external parties are linked either by data, processes, or people.

## *Profiling Information for External Value Chain Communications*

> ○ Who will be appointed as technical liaison between the organization and its upstream suppliers?
>
> ○ Who will be appointed as technical liaison between the organization and its downstream customers?
>
> ○ Who will be appointed as business and change liaison between the organization and its upstream suppliers?
>
> ○ Who will be appointed as business and change liaison between the organization and its downstream customers?
>
> ○ How will project information be communicated and shared?
>
> ○ How will project communications such as group meetings, one-on-one meetings, online forums, blogs, emails, memos, or any other appropriate communication channels be conducted.

Always make sure decisions and agreements are recorded and disseminated to the parties involved.

## Vendor Communications

A communications strategy must be in place when a vendor is appointed. This strategy should establish and define the reporting lines between the organization, the vendor and external customers and suppliers. It should also extend to any other incumbent vendors involved in the implementation where integration between the new system and incumbents is required.

## Communications and Requirements Gathering

When establishing vendor communication channels, it is important to identify and articulate what the vendor's "decision rights" are in relation to their authority to make project decisions about the 'who, what, when, and how' required for IT system changes. By imposing a formal communications structure and appointing single points of contact to communicate technical and business issues with each party, the risk of fragmented, undocumented, unshared and unaccountable cross-divisional communications between the organization, vendors, customers and suppliers is significantly reduced.

New IT systems often require some level of integration with incumbent systems or changes in the specifications. Therefore, the appropriate people from vendors and the organization must be appointed to ensure this important work is not overlooked. Prior to appointing a vendor or services supplier, ensure that the organization has appointed a single technical and business contact to liaise between the organization, the new vendor, and any incumbent vendors or providers. An organization should also insist that the new and incumbent vendors appoint primary technical and business contacts who will liaise with the organization's appointees. This will improve accountability by clarifying who is to be involved in formal project communications with these parties.

## *Profiling Information for Vendor Communications*

○ Who will be appointed as technical liaison between the organization and its vendors? New Vendor, Incumbent Vendor 1, 2, 3, 4, 5, 6

○ Who from each of the vendors will be appointed as the technical liaison with the organization? New Vendor, Incumbent Vendor 1, 2, 3, 4, 5, 6

○ Who will be appointed as the business liaison between the organization and its vendors? New Vendor, Incumbent Vendor 1, 2, 3, 4, 5, 6

○ Who from each of the vendors will be appointed as the business liaison with the organization? New Vendor, Incumbent Vendor 1, 2, 3, 4, 5, 6

○ How will project information be communicated?

○ Identify appropriate communication channels such as group meetings, one-on-one meetings, online forums, blogs, emails, memos, or any other appropriate communication channel

## Gathering Requirements

Gathering requirements to scope an IT system that satisfies all of an organization's needs relies primarily on a comprehensive communication strategy. This strategy will ensure that the project's scope and requirements are correctly and collaboratively defined by the organization and that internal and external user requirements are asked for and gathered from the appropriate sources.

The following communications must take place during the requirements gathering phase.

# Communications and Requirements Gathering

(1) The organization's strategic objectives, expectations, success, and progress metrics must be communicated to business and IT

(2) Business and user requirements and current processes must be identified, documented, and communicated to the organization and IT

(3) IT infrastructure capabilities, estimated human resources, and project time frames must be communicated to business and senior executives.

By successfully and comprehensively documenting and communicating the above, subsequent communications are more likely to be based on accurate and factual information. This reduces the probability of creating confusion or ambiguity between what the organization, business, user departments, IT department and selected vendor/s expect.

Since the majority of subsequent project implementation communications involve the vendor, their perception and understanding of what the system should deliver will be based on the organization's documented and mutually agreed upon requirements. Extensive, accurate, and factual requirements gathering is essential, therefore, since they are the foundation of the project's scope and deliverables. If an organization's Request for Proposal (RFP) is inaccurate or incomplete, then the vendor's initial understanding of the requirements will also be inaccurate. The chances of the end system not delivering what the organization expects is then almost guaranteed and correcting omissions and inaccuracies along the way will be an expensive and arduous exercise.

## Stop Blaming the Software

Gaining a broad and incisive view of the entire organization and its external value chain and proper identification of all direct and indirect relationship and communication channels that exist will significantly increase an organization's chances of getting their requirements and project scope right the first time.

## Documenting Requirements

Although an RFP is required for sizable new IT projects, not every IT investment necessarily involves an RFP. However, when a project does require an RFP, if requirements have not been gathered extensively from appropriately identified sources and the RFP is then issued prematurely, the implementation will be doomed before it gets off the ground.

Before putting pen to paper, proposing functionality and specifying unsubstantiated requirements, analysis of the organization's profile will ensure that requirements have been sourced from all parts of the organization as well as its external value chain that will be impacted by the system. This also means the project will be substantiated by business needs rather than being driven by the IT solution. Although the IT department provides the technical specifications and infrastructure required for an IT project, any technical objections should be carefully vetted and business must not be led astray by unsubstantiated IT objections. A project must be business led rather than IT driven.

To document "business driven" requirements without getting bogged down in the IT technicalities, it is often better that requirements are written by business managers, with the IT department providing input regarding IT-related matters.

## Communications and Requirements Gathering

These business managers will not know all of the business requirements, but having profiled the organization, they will be able to identify where and from whom to source business, user, and external requirements.

Finally, be aware that leaving communications to spontaneously occur between the CIO or IT department and the business or strategic planning department is in itself a high risk. These important communications probably won't even happen if left to chance because IT is often too far removed from these people and departments. It is imperative an organization facilitates collaboration and collective decision making and ensures communication channels between these departments are established upfront, with those responsible for project communications being appointed at the outset.

# CHAPER

# 13

# Gaining Support
for
the Project

*"Lead, follow, or get out of the way"*
Thomas Paine

## Gaining Support for the Project

The decision to invest in a new IT system must have full executive, management, and stakeholder support as well as the support of the entire organization and users who will be affected.

Chief Executives often incorrectly assume strategic investment decisions are to be made by them alone and that simply communicating these decisions to management and staff will suffice. However, all too often different levels of management and executives who have either not been involved in project decisions or have not been invited to provide their input into system requirements "appear" to be in support of the decision when, in truth, they are only paying lip-service. The quality of their input into requirements is therefore likely to be poor, minimal, and loosely defined because they feel it is someone else's project, not theirs.

How do we know? Because when things suddenly start to go askew, there are generally more executives and managers nay saying than those trying to rectify the situation or support those directly involved in getting the project back on track.

Why is this so? The answer can often be linked directly to one of the following criteria:

(a) Executives and managers were not held accountable for their decisions and just went along anyway because it was easier to agree than disagree

(b) An "I don't care because I was not/am not involved" attitude

(c) The investment decision was not based upon substantial quality input from appropriate sources

(d) If decision makers were not held accountable for the quality of their decisions, often the quality of input and information upon which they have based their decisions is incorrect and incomplete or poor at best

(e) Gaining manager and user support was merely a canvassing exercise conducted by senior executives to give the impression they are doing the right thing, making themselves feel better, and ultimately giving themselves an alibi if things go wrong down the track

As correct as it may be for senior management to make IT investment decisions, they still need to ensure they have the full support of their management teams and staff. Therefore, before making the final investment decision, all appropriate managers need to be identified to ensure that they do, in fact, support the project. This is easily achieved using an organization's profile to identify the direct and indirect executives, managers, and channels whose support for the project is required from start to finish.

An organization's profile is also a tool for executives and managers to identify whose support they need to gain and from where they need to gather input and system requirements.

# Gaining Support for the Project

## Gaining Support through Accountability

One of the most difficult tasks senior executives need to accomplish at the outset of an IT project is to assign accountability to all of the major players. This needs to be achieved without setting up scapegoats or preparing to duck for cover when difficulties arise.

Delegating responsibility will not necessarily lead to improving the quality of corporate decisions, whereas assigning full accountability does. Although this is not always the case, many IT implementation failures can be attributed to incomplete requirements, changing requirements, a lack of communications, and project scope-creep. These issues arose when those tasked with sourcing project requirements were not diligent or rigorous enough in performing their tasks because they were only responsible, rather than accountable.

Those tasked with sourcing project requirements who base their strategy on incorrect assumptions, rather than direct knowledge, often mistakenly believe they fully understand their organization's needs and what the users want. By making them fully accountable, such issues are much less likely to arise because they are more likely to obtain complete, extensive, and quality input knowing they will have to answer directly if requirements are incorrect or incomplete.

Often managers and executives accept responsibilities knowing that accountability ultimately lies with their seniors. However, by making the people who are directly tasked with supplying critical information and requirements fully accountable rather than just responsible, an organization will increase the quality of its input into requirements and at the same time gain ongoing project support from those involved.

Additionally, it will also ensure that the organization is able to disseminate accurate and salient information to all parties (users, departments, customers, suppliers, and vendors).

Executives and managers can then also assign accountability for tasks to their subordinates (rather than just delegating responsibility) because salient information and complete and accurate input must be sourced directly from them. Even those in junior positions have valuable input into project requirements, and if they are not solicited for their input or are not involved in decisions that relate to their work, they will naturally feel excluded and will have a lack of ownership for the system.

With no "skin in the game," they will also be less inclined to fully adopt, utilize, or support the system. User acceptance is a vitally important aspect of adoption to ensure the final production system is fully utilized to deliver the expected end results. This level of acceptance is directly influenced by the communication channels an organization employs for end users.

A corporate profile will immediately identify the best communication sources as well as those parties and end users who need to be identified and targeted for input into the project's requirements.

## *Profiling Information for Gaining Executive Support for the Project*

> o Has support for the project been secured from all C-Level executives, senior executives, managers, project managers, IT stakeholders, customers, and suppliers? Identify the people from each category who support the project

> ○ Are these people accountable for their input and decisions or are they simply responsible?
>
> ○ How has their support been secured?
>
> ○ What, in particular, are their reasons for supporting this project and what have they done to demonstrate their support rather than simply stating it?
>
> ○ What specifically is being done to ensure their ongoing support for the project?

## Gaining User Support and Adopting the System

Project specifications are often based on what an organization wants to achieve at a strategic level and what a select few at the top of the organization believe the user requirements are. However, when the system goes live, it's the level of user satisfaction that will determine its success. Therefore, if the system lacks what is required at their level and they do not feel the change was worthwhile for the job function, the project will not fully achieve the organization's objectives. Soliciting and including user input to formulate system requirements at the project's inception will, therefore, ensure a user-friendly and fully functional system that satisfies their requirements. It will also ensure that "user ownership" is established early on in the project.

A corporate profile will ensure that requirements and what the organization expects to achieve at all levels are identified. Additionally, input and suggestions from users must also be included, where appropriate, and management must acknowledge these inclusions so users will feel a sense of ownership for contributing to the system. More often than not IT staff design important aspects, such as the user interface of a new system, with little if any input from the users themselves. Although IT and management may consider the interface to be intuitive and easy to use, in reality it may not match the workflow or may miss elements that are vital to end users.

Failure to involve users in discussions or not asking for their input may result in subtle sabotaging or under-utilization of the system on their part. Often, organizations and senior management operate under the illusion that because they manage the company and its employees, they control how the system will be adopted. Chances are these senior executives' attitudes will be that they will "insist" that their users adopt and utilize the system "exactly as planned." Unfortunately, it is inevitably the users, albeit in a subtle way, who decide on how smoothly the implementation will proceed and how easy it will be for an organization to assimilate the system.

### Profiling Information for Gaining User Support and Adoption

> o Has support for the project been secured from all internal and external users (incumbent and new system users)?
>
> o What specifically has been done to gain and secure their support?
>
> o What has been done to ensure their adoption of the system?
>
> o How has the organization involved its users in the project?
>
> o How are communications with all the users conducted?

# Gaining Support for the Project

> o What feedback mechanisms are in place for handling project queries and input from users (both pre-and post-implementation)?
>
> o Are the users (incumbent and new system users) accountable for their project input and requirements or are they simply responsible? Explain.
>
> o Has adequate training been factored in to ensure all users will be competent in the use of the new system?
>
> o Has the organization communicated to them the impact on their operations when they convert to the new system?

## Management's Influence on User Adoption

Considering the impact that factors such as employee resistance to change, user involvement, and organizational culture have on the outcome of an IT implementation, the following management factors can influence a project's success.

(a) Attitudes towards the system by C-Level executives, managers, users, customers, and other stakeholders

(b) Management and executive support for the project

(c) Appropriate and timely user involvement

(d) Complete training, development, and confirmed system acceptance

(e) End-user adoption

## Stop Blaming the Software

Since the success of an IT implementation ultimately depends on how well the system is adopted by end users, an organization and its senior executives need to be constantly mindful of how these management factors positively or negatively impact its adoption. If users "perceive" that management's attitude and support for the system is weak, or if management fails to secure their involvement at the outset, end-user support for the system will diminish as will their desire to utilize and fully adopt the system.

# CHAPTER 14

# Managing Change

*"The world hates change, yet it is the only thing that has brought progress"*

Charles Kettering

Organizations all hope their IT projects will not encounter internal or external resistance, but they also tend to simply assume they have everyone's support and agreement. They reason there should be no resistance to its execution because the benefits that the new IT system will deliver to the organization, its employees, and users far outweigh any temporary discomfort that may be experienced during the transition. Unfortunately, not all employees consider the benefits an organization will receive to be more important than the discomfort and change that they, their position, or job function will have to undergo. They often openly state their agreement or support for the decision whilst harboring silent opposition or contempt, or simply agreeing for expedient reasons.

## Identifying and Overcoming Resistance to Change

Accepting that resistance to change is inevitable enables an organization to identify where resistance is legitimate, what resistance is cultural, or whether it is a socially constructed belief system. Acknowledging legitimate resistance allows employees' specific concerns to be addressed at the outset of the project rather than letting resistance grow and take hold.

# Stop Blaming the Software

Reasons for resistance to change can be caused by any of the following:

- **Excluded**—Executives, managers, and users who believe they were left out of vital decision-making processes will erect obstacles to prevent or hinder the project because they were kept in the "dark" (the mushroom syndrome).
- **Fear of the unknown**—Management and employees feel insecure or unsafe in their positions and not in control of upcoming events and changes.
- **Lack of understanding and communications**—Organizational reasons to support, validate, and justify the IT project have not been clearly communicated to management and employees so they do not understand the legitimacy of the project.
- **Self absorbed**—Executives and managers may oppose the new IT system because they feel their positions are threatened and that the system will downgrade or erode their perceived power base.
- **Thinly veiled contempt (TVC)**—When an individual, a department, or indeed an entire community is held in contempt due to discriminating factors, although no-one overtly shows their contempt, they nevertheless disregard any ideas or suggestions from such parties. As a result, it appears that everyone supports the change, but in actual fact this is not the true situation.

By identifying and profiling these pockets of resistance before the project starts, an organization can take action to either minimize resistance or to lock-in support. Encouraging employee participation by asking for their input, empowering them, setting objectives or visioning at the outset is a very effective way to decrease resistance and increase support for change. By being involved in the change, their feelings of insecurity and lack of control are minimized and mitigated. Unfortunately, by waiting until the project is underway, overcoming resistance or identifying pockets of resistance becomes increasingly difficult.

Additionally, assessing the level of participation in the change will also be an indication of their support or resistance. If resistance to change persists, an organization can "command" the change. However, it is better to firstly secure support from the majority of the organization or to ensure some of those resistant to change have been converted into those who support change.

Many of these reasons for resistance to change can be overcome through:

- Honest, effective, and timely organizational communications and feedback. People don't like bad news but prefer that to being manipulated or deceived
- Involving and empowering employees early in the project to get them to actively participate in the change process
- Conveying the vision for the project and enrolling people to pursue it
- Acknowledging and managing legitimate concerns
- Using a "Pull" (encouraging) rather than a "Push" (forcing) motivation for the change, which includes using clear goals and objectives
- Motivating people and departments to change through attractive incentives rather than fear and coercion (although

these can be used as a last resort, particularly when timing is a factor)

Individuals who support change are often those who are reliant or dependent on certain people, or departments that have elevated themselves to informal "self-appointed" positions of power and control. Even though these supportive individuals rely on those self-appointed parties to function, they do not enjoy or benefit from the social transaction. They will, therefore, welcome the opportunity to be released from such dependencies. In fact, they are likely to relish the demise of these self-appointed power holders. These people support change because they see it as a way to get away from a particular informal power structure.

When self-appointed power holders are moved out of their comfort zone, their resistance to change is often disguised by the following:

- **DeadWood**—these are people who have been with an organization for many years and perform their tasks extremely well. They are reluctant to share their hard-won knowledge because they fear losing power, control, and security when their power base of knowledge becomes obsolete.
- **Stuck in the Past Mentality**—The "that's the way we do things around here" mentality is often the "going-in" attitude of lazy individuals who can't be bothered or consider themselves superior to their peers and are unwilling to adapt to change. Unfortunately, this attitude often infects other departments, groups, or teams and can become widespread, especially amongst those who believe they or their teams are indispensable. Their perceived power base relies upon

the status quo, thereby posing a great risk that needs to be dealt with firmly otherwise it will retard progress and put the entire project at risk.

All of an organization's functions, departments, parties, and people that are involved in the change will have already been identified through the corporate profile. Potential pockets of resistance or support for the change can then be located and further profiling of communication channels will also help to identify change supporters or resisters as indicated by their level of input, communications, and feedback. This will also highlight the organization's components and users that should be involved at the outset in order to mitigate against resistance to change and foster and maintain their support.

## Profiling Information for Elements of Resistance and Support

These are the parties and people that have already been identified as either being involved with, needing to be involved, or are required to provide input into the project. Which of these parties or people in particular appear reluctant to change or are resistant to or supportive of the change?

---

- o  Project Sponsor
- o  IT investment decision makers
- o  Stakeholders not involved with the investment decision
- o  C-level executives or senior executives not involved with the investment decision
- o  Functions, business units, or departments

---

> - Functions, business units or department managers or executives
> - Internal users of the incumbent system
> - Intended internal users of the new system
> - External users of the incumbent system
> - Intended external users of the new system
>
> Give reasons for selecting any of the above.

Another fundamental factor to consider when undertaking organizational change is that the "soft" and intangible nature of an organization's culture cannot easily be mapped, readily identified, or quickly changed. It is, however, still something the management team needs to seriously consider for management and control very early on in the IT investment decision-making process.

When most people in an organization are either stuck in the past or operate only in the present with no vision for the future, they will naturally resist new ideas and change. This is often an indication that the organization's culture is being influenced by either the Business Owners, Senior Executives, CEO, Founders, or Industry. This is not to say all Senior Executives, CEOs, or Founders create and influence a change—resistant culture, but by being in a position of power and control and being responsible for creating, influencing, and supporting this culture, their actions will determine whether the entire organization is either resistant to change, supportive of it, or are instigators of change.

Many of the mental and cultural roadblocks an organization's employees, departments, or groups may inadvertently erect are due to factors such as:

- A socially constructed belief system
- Stuck in the good old days and ways
- Group-think occurring within groups or departments

Often senior executives and employees have different opinions of their organization's culture. Consequently, unless everyone in the organization agrees about its culture, culture management will become haphazard and ultimately put the project at risk.

## *Profiling Information for Corporate Culture*

These questions need to be posed to each relevant person without collaboration with peers.

| |
|---|
| o What type of corporate culture do the C-Level executives say the organization has? C-Level 1, C-Level 2, C-Level 3 etc. |
| o How do Senior Executives define the organization's culture? Executive 1, executive 2, executive 3 etc. |
| o How does middle management define the organization's culture? Manager 1, manager 2, manager 3 etc. |
| o How do the employees define the organization's culture? One employee from within each function or business unit |
| o Do all those on the same level agree? If not, how are they different? |
| o Do all levels agree? If not, how are they different? |

# Stop Blaming the Software

## Getting to the starting blocks

All IT implementations involve organizational change to some extent and all change requires organization-wide support. Whether changing culture, processes, structure, or strategy, all will require the same level of diligence, involvement, and support for the change to be successful.

Change is a complex and arduous process and should not be undertaken lightly or without a comprehensive plan. Because IT change often requires extensive organizational change, the organization needs to be able to identify from its profile where the organizational elements, processes, and people are interconnected. This allows accurate identification of what needs to be changed pre-implementation and who needs to be involved when. By only identifying elements at a high level rather than identifying and recognizing the critical role the elements' interconnectedness plays in change will put a project at risk. Failing to identify even a single link or assuming it is not important to the project can be a fatal omission.

## The Change Process

Organization change frameworks and processes will vary from company to company, with many using in-house developments based upon their experience or frameworks that have evolved from their original form. However, whichever framework or process an organization uses, all change requires a rigorous and comprehensive process that identifies and encompasses all relevant organizational components, as well as a plan for moving the organization from its current scenario through the change, to finally anchoring the change in the organization.

# Managing Change

The change frameworks and processes discussed in this chapter are used primarily to demonstrate "Who," "What," "How," and "Why," is involved with, and impacted by, IT change. Although they are very good examples, I am not suggesting these are necessarily the preferred models for change. Being proficient and diligent at administering change frameworks and processes requires a high level of expertise and hands-on experience that not all organizations possess (let alone managers having sufficient time to ensure the change process is properly adhered to and monitored). Since organizations will undergo dramatic changes when an IT project is instigated, they need to be able to identify where, who, and what within the organization will change and to know beforehand how they plan to manage and control the changes.

Change frameworks and methodologies can be either process or factor based. In process-based frameworks, the steps either follow a logical or sequential order, whilst the factors determining the implementation success criteria are based on sociological and technological factors. IT project change frameworks require a balance of socio-technical factors to succeed because by focusing only on the technical aspect of the implementation, the organization is unlikely to pay enough attention to the sociological aspect of change.

Paying due attention to the sociological aspect of change will ensure stakeholders, users, and management are prepared for change, recognize, and support the need for change and, as a consequence, are more likely to adopt the proposed system. As technical as IT system implementations are, it is the sociological aspects that can prove pivotal to the outcome since it is a lack of communications, support, and rapport that have been proven to be critical to the success of many projects. The converse is also true. If the sociological aspects of a project overshadow attention to its technical aspects, then the potential success of an implementation is likely to be compromised.

## Change frameworks

"The Diamond Model" for change conceptualizes the organization as a diamond consisting of four components, all of which interact with each other and hence influence each other to change.

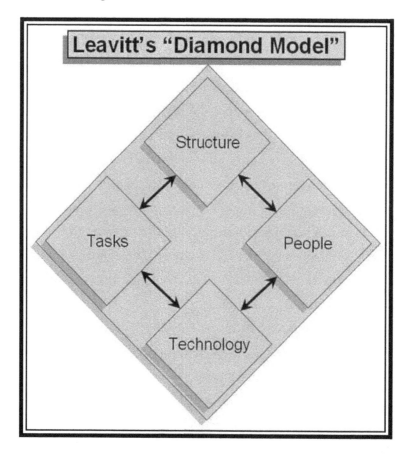

**Source: Adapted from Leavitt's (1965) 'Diamond Model'.**

# Managing Change

A major change such as changing or redefining an organization's strategy will often drive the organization's decision to invest in new IT systems. Consequently, this type of change affects all sides of the diamond, thereby requiring people, structure, technology, and tasks to change in order to support the overall change.

Since an IT implementation is not an isolated project, it should not be treated as such, and therefore the entire organization needs to be readied and included in the change so they can embrace and support it. The organization's functions, processes and people that have already been identified through previous profiling phases are the starting points for identifying specifically who and what will be impacted by the change, who needs to be involved and when.

It is also imperative to identify at the outset the less obvious components of an organization and its external value chain that the IT implementation will either directly or indirectly impact or affect. By identifying what, where, and who will influence the final outcome and how, the amount of attention they require can then be determined and when their involvement will be needed.

Lewin's "Unfreezing, Moving, Refreezing" model starts off by unfreezing the organization for the changes ahead. This is done by unfreezing the current situation or status quo and identifying change-resistant components. This is based upon the notion that the two opposing force fields, (a) resistance and (b) support for change, need to be identified and addressed.

| Unfreezing | Moving | Refreezing |
|---|---|---|

**Source: Adopted from Lewin's three-stage classic change model**

# Stop Blaming the Software

The unfreezing phase is the most unstable of the three phases, because it brings out the majority of people's resistance and discomfort because change involves them moving out of their comfort zones. This move is seldom easy because even though people enjoy talking about change and envisioning the future, it does not necessarily mean they will change without the organization encouraging or motivating them to do so.

The unfreezing stage emphasizes the critical nature that Diagnosing, Visioning, and Planning plays in change and that without it an organization's strategy, vision or strategic intent, cannot be formulated.

(a) Diagnosis—Where are we now? Assess the organization's current scenario or situation
(b) Visioning—As an organization, where do we want to be in the future? Develop a scenario for what the organization envisions the future will look like
(c) Planning—What needs to be done to get there? Develop a plan and strategies for moving towards the future

The moving step is the journey of transitioning the organization through the necessary changes in order to undertake the IT project implementation. This phase is typified by the collective organization being in a constant state of either flux or limbo because nothing appears to be permanent or stable. This temporary environment often fosters an attitude of lack of accountability, lack of responsibility or not knowing what to do or how to perform tasks because they have changed.

During the moving phase, an organization needs to adopt appropriate mechanisms, processes, and controls to drive and support the change. Most of the staff, departments, and functions will by now have recognized and increasingly accepted the need for change. All being well, the organization's components and people that were identified and profiled as potentially resisting change will now have been converted to supporters of change.

The 'refreezing' phase is based on the concept of permanency, which is required for change to be successful.

Permanency means not reverting to the way things were before or returning to an old way of doing things. It creates a situation of organizational consistency and stability. It is the permanent nature of the change that enables and sustains it to become entrenched and integrated, and it is an ongoing process that is anchored within the organization. Bear in mind though, that rather than attempting to apply permanence to a constantly evolving IT environment, organizations need to remain agile enough to be able to move and adapt to new and emergent technologies rather than becoming encumbered by a rigid process for the sake of permanency. It will, therefore, be the relevance of the change or new IT system that determines the duration for which permanency can be maintained.

# CHAPTER

# 15

# Solution and Vendor Selection Framework

*"Facts do not cease to exist because they are ignored"*
Aldous Huxley

# Solution and Vendor Selection Framework

Having profiled the organization and gathered all of the business requirements from appropriate sources, the organization can now discern what "must" be included as functionality, as opposed to the "should haves" and "nice to haves." These top-priority business requirements will then determine what technical capabilities the solution needs. Whether they are a package implementation or a bespoke development, the following criteria must be included in the decision-making framework for selecting a solution and vendor or systems integrator.

## Vendor Selection and Management

Vendor selection is a critical decision, and the following sections call for vendor analysis, vendor selection criteria, and identifying what must be included in their solution.

All too often the decision to select a vendor is based on the current incumbent provider, the lowest quote, the best known supplier, or because the vendor is a friend or acquaintance of an executive. A vendor must always be selected based on their core business being in the system, service, or technology they are proposing.

# Stop Blaming the Software

Although the most economical proposal has a good chance of winning an organization's business, be aware some costs may be hidden due to incomplete or inaccurate requirements. As additions or changes are identified later in the project, scope-creep will increase the vendor's revenue at the organization's expense. Therefore, an organization is better off using its corporate profile to identify all requirements upfront before requesting vendor proposals.

Other than the obvious commercial criteria, the two most important questions to consider in selecting a vendor are:

(a) Is implementing the software package, software development, consulting service, or technology (whatever the case may be) their core strength and main business focus?

(b) Have the organization's requirements been extensively, rigorously, and accurately profiled to ensure the proposal includes all the "must have" requirements?

To identify a reputable and appropriate vendor who is the right fit for an organization and one who can address the project's requirements, a close analysis of the vendor organization is recommended, rather than just going with the market leader or most widely recognized vendor. Just because the vendor is large or well known within the industry does not automatically mean that vendor is the correct choice for an organization; nor does it mean the vendor is necessarily the best in its field. Organizations should take into account that vendors often agree to undertake IT projects they assume are fully scoped and properly specified by their customer, but which they later discover are inaccurate in terms of the scope and requirements.

# Solution and Vendor Selection Framework

Vendor selection is another point in the pre-implementation decision-making process an organization must approach with rigor. Being accountable for the choice of a vendor requires the organization to undertake a critical vendor analysis. This analysis must be undertaken pre-investment to identify which vendors are prepared to make the effort to carefully consider and respond to the organization's requirements proving they do, in fact, specialize in the applicable software solutions, development, or implementation as their core business function, rather than as a secondary business focus. A few large hardware and consulting organizations have diversified into software development and implementation through acquisitions. These vendors may look promising as one-stop shops but be aware that during these acquisitions a lot of expertise will have been lost due to restructuring, resizing, and redundancies. A transfer of knowledge and expertise before resizing may mean they no longer have the focus, knowledge, or the expertise the organization may require for its project.

Mandating a single-source supplier to minimize the number of vendor relationships an organization needs to manage is a common practice but it can also be a costly mistake. By outsourcing both software and hardware requirements to a single vendor, knowing the vendor's core competency is in providing only part of the solution will not be in the organization's best interests. Consequently, if a vendor does agree to take on the software development or implementation, they may not be able to provide the expertise and necessary resources required. A smaller company specializing in the system the organization is seeking or where software development is their main focus may be a better fit because it is their core competency.

# Stop Blaming the Software

Obviously, if the vendor is too small, it will mean they will not be able to provide sufficient resources for the implementation or to support the system into the future. Conversely, a large organization may not be able to provide the level of customer intimacy an organization requires if they are too thinly spread across too many projects. During the project life cycle, they may not be willing or able to provide the necessary customer intimacy or direct sufficient attention to the project due to a distorted "superiority" attitude.

Either of the above scenarios will hinder communications between them and the organization as well between other vendors and suppliers. Unless an organization has clearly defined communication channels, with appropriate people appointed to facilitate communications between the organization and vendors, both incumbent and new, vendors will often not communicate with each other and won't share potential project problems and solutions.

During my interview with a large telecommunications organization, it became apparent that incorrect vendor selection, lack of communications, and inaccurate requirements were prevalent in one of their IT projects. The project had been established to integrate a new system into their existing systems to bypass the incumbent vendor's proprietary systems interface. However, the incumbent vendor refused to communicate with the new vendor or with the customer about the specifications of the proprietary interface.

Their initial prototype system seemed to work but the production system was subject to extensive ongoing modifications and redevelopment, resulting in a final system that was a far cry from what the organization had expected. These modifications were due to the organization failing to identify a lack of robust and extensive requirements. Although the initially agreed KPI's to determine the project's success were never achieved, the system was functional and therefore put into production.

These project problems were partially due to the vendors' lack of understanding of the software requirements, which indicates poor communications between the organization and its vendors. The vendor agreed to undertake the software development even though their primary business was in consulting services and hardware sales. They were chosen because they were the organization's incumbent hardware vendor, which showed that the organization was trying to consolidate the number of vendor relationships they needed to manage by seeking a one-stop vendor. The organization later regarded the vendor as having poor communication skills, poor client relationship skills, and a lack of commitment to the implementation, and attributed all of the problems to this vendor who, in turn, believed it was beyond reproach.

Analyzing the vendor will identify proficiencies or deficiencies in:

- Implementing off-the-shelf proven solutions
- Implementing package solutions with customizations
- Bespoke development (software developed to specifications)
- IT consulting (how to)
- IT project management (doing and managing)
- Hardware and infrastructure
- Technical and user training

# Stop Blaming the Software

## Vendor Selection Criteria

Vendor selection is a rigorous process and a decision that requires serious thought because the organization will rely on it now and in the future. As with selecting the right solution, vendors must also be matched according to an organization's specific needs. Rather than realizing only after the point of no return that their solution does not match the organization's requirements or that the vendor is not an appropriate "fit" for the organization, the selection criteria will assist in making the 'right fit' choice at the outset.

When investing in a new IT system, cost and expenditure budget will likely be one of the top priorities. To stay within budget, organizations may be tempted to cut corners or to trim costs such as vendor training. Although training may appear to be excessively expensive, training users to operate and use the system proficiently will pay dividends when it comes to user adoption. Training empowers the users, increases their confidence, and, more importantly, allows the organization to get maximum efficiency and return from its investment due to its competence and rapid adoption. Bedding-down issues are also quickly identified because the system is being widely used by competent users.

## Profiling Information for Vendor and Solution Selection

- o Is their core business the product or service that is being invested in?
- o Are they the right fit for the organization?
- o Do the full project costs and overall budget include training, maintenance and support, licensing fees, documentation, testing, account management, plus additional hardware as required?

- o Is the prospective vendor's long-term viability sound, and if the company is in acquisition mode, will its focus on the solution be at risk?
- o How can the prospective vendor confirm it is committed to supporting its product or service solution over the anticipated life of the system?
- o How does the vendor "future proof" its solution with upgrades and new releases, and has the full cost of this maintenance been factored in?
- o Reference customers: Check all prospective vendors' backgrounds, including case studies and basic product information, as well as their proven capabilities in delivering on schedule and according to the requirements. Most importantly, confirm the people they will assign to the project have sufficient knowledge.
- o Is their training and support offering satisfactory?
- o Confirm their capability to communicate well at all levels and that they have good interpersonal skills (especially good listening skills).

## Managing the Vendor

Selecting a vendor is only the first of many steps in the vendor-client relationship. Managing the vendor and their relationship then becomes an important ongoing task. The following caveats need to be established and rigorously adhered to to ensure an organization manages its project and vendors and not the other way around.

# Stop Blaming the Software

(1) Ensure the organization has clearly documented and articulated exactly what it expects the system to deliver, based upon precise and extensive organizational and user requirements.

(2) Ensure the organization retains ownership of the implementation and drives the process rather than relinquishing project ownership to the vendor/system implementer, thereby empowering the vendor to drive the process.

(3) Establish clear communication channels and appoint specific person/s to liaise between the organization, vendor, incumbent vendors, stakeholders, and any other third parties involved.

(4) Ensure an SLA is binding and ensure all legalities are covered to minimize IT risk exposure.

Once an organization has gathered its requirements and appointed vendors and system implementers, it can be tempted to relinquish control and accountability for the IT implementation to the vendor or another third party because it perceives them to be the experts. However, it is the organization's money at stake and everyone's reputation is on the line. Therefore, the organization needs to remain in control and rigorously manage the vendor to ensure it stays abreast of the project's progress and deals with issues when they arise.

Vendor management is always a learning curve for all parties, especially where there have previously been bad experiences. Be warned that if the organization does not manage its vendor it will risk the vendor taking control and managing the project to its own standards and timeframes.

# Solution and Vendor Selection Framework

Alternatively, if the budget allows, one may appoint a VMO (Vendor Management Organization) to manage vendors and to assist with the IT investment decision. Considering that VMOs interact with IT vendors regularly and have a strong current knowledge of vendors and their solutions, they are often better placed to negotiate pricing, quality, vendor commitment, and expertise and to select a solution that's aligned with business initiatives. This also enables the organization to actively manage risk if its capability or expertise in vendor and contract management is deficient.

Since many vendors have diversified their product and service offerings by bundling consulting services with hardware and software (for example, HP's merger with EDS), a more thorough knowledge of technology to address an organization's requirements is required when making an IT investment. Bear in mind that vendors invariably sell their solutions based on features and functionality, rather than what is actually needed. Consequently, it is easy to be overwhelmed and dazzled by science shifting the focus away from what the organization actually needs.

When selecting a vendor and solution it is imperative to constantly refer back to the organization's requirements that were identified from its profile. They need to constantly check back to confirm that the functionality or features that are being agreed to are those that were specified in the initial requirements documentation. If these are not in the initial specification, the organization needs to question whether they should have been there in the first place or whether they are inadvertently creating project scope-creep. Will it be a feature or function that is paid for but never used?

# CHAPTER

# 16

# Training
# and
# Development

*"Folklore and rumor are inadequate means of spreading
information about how to use a computer system"*
John Gustafson

# Training and Development

Often IT investment decisions are made to match planned investment costs with the cost of the solution. By doing this, organizations will invariably omit important but not so obvious costs such as product and process training from the project's budget. IT solution investment costs must include comprehensive vendor-supplied system training and process and business training. At the completion of a project an organization may not be able to free up resources without making sacrifices elsewhere, so this must also be included upfront in its training budget.

## User training

If users do not receive sufficient formal training in the new system, the system will not be used to its full capacity and will be poorly adopted. Therefore, at the time of making the investment decision, the organization needs to plan ahead, be prepared to invest heavily in user training, and not be tempted to penny-pinch.

To increase the probability of an IT implementation succeeding, these three critical training issues must be fully addressed:

(1) Does the initial investment cost include product, system, business, and process training for all those involved? If it does not, then the organization needs to ensure it has budgeted sufficiently for all vendor supplied and other relevant training.

(2) Ensure an appropriate education and training program is established to explain to employees how the new system will work and what changes will impact upon them and the organization.

(3) Perform a "Training gap analysis." Do users require additional training to enhance their use of the system? For example, when implementing a new CRM or Sales Automation system, do they require additional sales training, up-selling techniques, or any other technical expertise?

In the absence or lack of system-specific training or business process training, users will often become resentful of the system and contemptuous towards the organization and those involved in implementing the system. These are critical factors that can result in a lack of user adoption thereby creating a technology mismatch whereby the new system is viewed as a 'white elephant.' User adoption and user satisfaction with the system can be increased by implementing a comprehensive system training and development plan for all users. This must also provide them with training for any additional technical, sales, or other business-related skills they may need to help them use the system effectively. Without these additional skills, the system is likely to be under-utilized. If the new system requires users to have additional knowledge about other applications, ensure that the appropriate training is delivered.

# Training and Development

As an example, the telecommunications organization mentioned earlier implemented a sales system but omitted to provide its staff with cross-selling and up-selling sales skills, resulting in them not achieving the results they expected from the system. In another example, an organization implemented a solution that required data to be imported via Microsoft Excel, but neglected to send their staff on Excel training courses. These organizations would both have benefited by either achieving increased telephone sales or having an easier bedding down process with less support costs had they provided additional training for their staff.

If the new system's user interface does not match the users' work-flow, is too convoluted, or insufficient training is provided, employees will inevitably create their own pen-and—paper methods for keeping track of information. The time and money the organization has invested in the new system will then not deliver a comprehensive single repository for vital company, customer, sales, employee, and historical information. An organization's knowledge and information can still walk out the door on a piece of paper or USB drive when employees resign. Additionally, an organization's ability to access and track historical information will be diminished.

## Profiling information for Training and Development

o    What is the training strategy for this project?
o    Has the cost of vendor-supplied system training and other relevant training been included in the budget? If not why not?
o    How will training be delivered? Online, one-on-one, group training, train the trainer or other, DVD, or manuals

- What additional training material will the vendor supply?
- Will Management and Senior Executives receive formal training?
- Will end users receive formal training?
- How sustainable is the training material post "go live"?
- Has the training schedule and rollout been planned for, and clearly communicated to, the organization?
- What additional training and skills are required for users' proficient employment of the system?
- What additional training is required for managers to understand the impact the system will have on operational procedures?
- What additional training and skills are required for executives to comprehend the functionality and benefits of the system?
- Is a methodology in place for conducting relevant training needs analysis at all levels of the organization?
- What additional training and skills are required for the IT department's proficient administration of the system?

# CHAPTER

# 17

# Succeeding at Corporate Profiling

*"You can have brilliant ideas, but if you can't get them across,*
*your ideas won't get you anywhere"*

Lee Iacocca

T he key to an organization's next IT project success will hinge upon how extensively and accurately the organization has been profiled. This book has discussed unbundling and profiling of an organization pre-implementation as well as profiling the major disciplines that need to be upheld to achieve an organization's objectives. This chapter summarizes the profiling concepts covered to create a conceptual framework for an organization's current and future IT projects.

Organizations should now realize scapegoating and targeting those who tried their best to deliver what was asked of them is a futile and counter-productive exercise, because the root causes of most failed IT projects are the exclusive domain of executive decision makers. Profiling relates to the strategic decisions and processes that should originate at the top of an organization. Therefore, if profiling is to stand a chance of being fully adopted and supported across an organization, the executive management team must already be 100% committed and support the success of the project at the outset.

The pre-investment IT Project Framework below is inclusive of a corporate profiling framework, as well as the pre-implementation strategies and decisions that cascade into the post-implementation review processes. This ensures that user adoption and organizational learning from the project's outcomes are achieved. This framework will also provide valuable historical data for future projects.

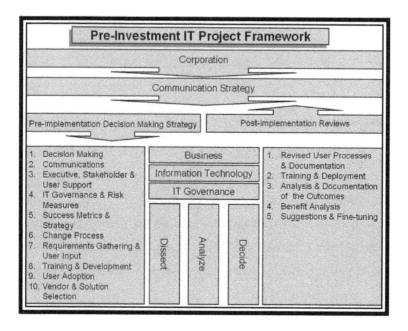

The Pre-investment IT Project Framework also encompasses a project's disciplines that need to be addressed pre-investment and undertaken pre-implementation. The organization's responses to profiling questions throughout this book will provide essential information and input that is required to feed into the rest of the pre-IT investment decision-making and pre-implementation processes.

The three key principles of corporate profiling, Visibility, Collaboration, and Accountability underpin the three integral elements of the Pre-investment IT Project Framework, namely Dissect (Unbundling), Analyze (Announce, Ask and Answer), Decide (Document and Do).

# Succeeding at Corporate Profiling

This framework uses information from an organization's profile to identify exactly which components of an organization need to be dissected and what needs to be analyzed and decided for the pre-implementation processes at the requirements gathering stages.

## Dissecting

Dissecting or unbundling an organization creates visibility into the interconnected relationships between functions, departments, processes, and people and whether these extend to the external value chain. If they do, it creates visibility into where, and identifies which, customers or suppliers need to be involved in the analysis phase. Visibility also enables an organization to accurately identify the (not so) obvious communication sources and channels, as well as being able to identify where the primary business and user project requirements need to be sourced. Visibility identifies where and from whom support for the investment and project implementation needs to be secured.

## Analyzing

An organization needs to start by announcing to its employees, stakeholders, and external customers or suppliers (that have been identified as requiring involvement in the project) the results of their investigations into the benefits of the proposed IT project. The organization needs to communicate to these parties that their collaboration and input is required to ensure the IT investment decisions are based on accurate, relevant, and all-inclusive information. This way, all parties are informed and included, and understand the organization's motives and objectives for the project. This approach helps to ensure these parties will be more likely to support the organization's IT investment decision and the project implementation.

An analysis of the unbundled organization and external value chain will identify the not-so-obvious relationships and interconnections that are often missed when communication and requirement sources for a project are being identified. This will also assist in identifying an organization's incumbent vendors that need to be included for system or process integration and project communications. Further analysis also enables identification of the less obvious but critical information, communication, input, and requirements sources. These are often left untapped because they either cannot be easily identified or because they are deemed to be irrelevant to the project. Analysis of the external industry value chain will also help to identify appropriate and best-fit vendors, suppliers, and system implementers.

Ask for input from everyone in the organization who will be involved in, or impacted by, the system as well as relevant external customers and suppliers to ensure the project requirements are accurate and relevant. Collaboration to determine relevance and to obtain an unbiased analysis of the project's requirements ensures that people feel involved in the decisions and are therefore more likely to support them.

Answer questions that arise during the preliminary investigations and planning processes. People like to be informed of changes, even at the proposal stages of a project, particularly if they believe they will be affected by them. By being open to answering questions about the pending change, the organization will also be able to gauge its readiness for change and to identify where possible pockets of support or resistance may lie.

## Decide

Based on an organization's corporate profile and the resulting analysis information, it must be decided which individuals will be accountable for making the many strategic project decisions. Accountability empowers decision makers, thereby improving the overall quality and support of their decisions.

Identify and decide who will be accountable for accurate and timely project communications with all relevant parties, people, and vendors. Further identify and decide who or what parties will be accountable for providing accurate requirements input and who will decide on the most compatible vendor for the organization. For example, deciding on which vendors will be requested to submit proposals is more likely to be correct where those accountable for gathering the requirements at the outset are made accountable for this task.

Documenting business and user requirements can only be done once an organization has been dissected and analyzed, because only then can complete, accurate, and extensive requirements be fully identified. This will provide the organization with a clear understanding of exactly what requirements the IT project needs to address to achieve the desired outcomes.

# CHAPTER

# 18

# Notable
# IT Project
# Failures

*"Failure is not a single, cataclysmic event. You don't fail overnight. Instead, failure is a few errors in judgment, repeated every day"*

Jim Rohn

# Notable IT Project Failures

## Microsoft—Windows Vista®

Since releasing Microsoft Windows® operating system for personal computers in November 1985, by mid May 2007 Microsoft's global market-share of both home and corporate users had grown to a staggering 92%. At that time, Microsoft's Chairman, Bill Gates, addressing the Windows Hardware Engineering Conference (WinHEC) in Los Angeles, reported that in just the first 100 days of general availability, Windows Vista® had managed to gather an installed base larger than that of Linux and Mac OS X combined.

Talking informally to reporters following his keynote address at CES 2007, Bill Gates was quoted as saying "Best $6 billion I ever spent. You don't need to feel bad for us in terms of the profitability of the Windows business. Did we learn? Yes. It's pretty exciting to see how the things we learned will let us do even better."

When Longhorn (the early code name for Windows Vista) was first announced in an article titled "A Fork in the Road to Longhorn?" in The Direction on Microsoft Web site on October 21, 2002, interim release dates of late 2004 or early 2005 were touted. This would make Windows Vista a full two years overdue. However, the real gauge of any project's success or otherwise is not just delivery on time. Where Windows Vista fell badly short of the mark was in terms of customer satisfaction and unmatched expectations. In these measures alone, Windows Vista falls into the failed IT Project category and here's why.

With a 92% global market share and Windows Vista pre-installed by computer manufacturers, it should come as no surprise that sales statistics showed Windows Vista to be a success, but in reality, that was just a natural effect of their market dominance. With their massive $6 billion Windows Vista project budget and millions of entrenched users already familiar with Microsoft Windows (and therefore not inclined to re-learn a different way of doing things even if the alternative is better), Microsoft's dominance with Windows Vista and its successor versions is unlikely to falter in the foreseeable future. Any other project that did not have such support or so much at stake would almost certainly have been euthanized because of (a) the massive budget blowout, (b) repeated missed deadlines, and most importantly (c), not meeting customer expectations.

The bottom line is that by virtue of its sheer market dominance, Microsoft succeeded with Windows Vista in spite of a clear lack of involvement and acknowledgement of its affected customers. In any other circumstances, the user community would have rejected the change from Windows XP to Windows Vista simply because (a) the change was too difficult and (b) there were no real reasons to make the change.

The following are three well documented examples of the shortfalls in Windows Vista at the time of its release:

(1) Microsoft Windows XP® (Windows Vista's predecessor) was backward compatible with previous Microsoft Windows

versions, but Windows Vista was not. Microsoft relied on third-party manufacturers to ensure their products were "Windows Vista Ready" but many software programs and hardware had not been upgraded when Windows Vista was finally released in January 2007. This meant many software programs and hardware (such as many popular USB MP3 players) that previously worked on Windows XP no longer worked on Windows Vista.

(2) Security setting using the new UAC (User Account Control) frustrated many home users, preventing them from modifying or accessing files as they could with previous versions. Not being able to access your data on your own personal computer was not a good welcome message to new users.

(3) Windows Vista is bloated with millions more lines of code than Windows XP. Rather than simplifying its use, Windows Vista required users to devote time and effort to come to terms with the new system. Although many of these features (such as the very useful, built-in search capability) are much needed improvements, but there just aren't enough compelling reasons for upgrading to Windows Vista.

Microsoft's dominance in PC operating systems may also prove to be a weakness. Consider their massive corporate profile spanning upstream and downstream value chains and their diverse global customer base. Ensuring requirements and needs are solicited from all of these affected parties while maintaining secrecy over their plans is an enormous undertaking. Windows 7, the successor to Windows Vista, was one of Microsoft's most secretive projects ever, and gathering diverse user requirements under those conditions has led to adoption issues similar to those Windows Vista faced.

This failure allowed Apple Computers to run a massively successful ad campaign ("I'm a Mac and I'm a PC") exploiting the negativity surrounding Windows Vista and its many failings. Google also picked up on this vulnerability and, following their successful inroads into the mobile phones market with their Android Operating System, Google has launched its own attack on the Netbook operating systems market (which by all rights should be dominated by Microsoft Windows™) with their planned Chrome Operating System.

The failure of Microsoft's Windows Vista project has allowed its competitors to make inroads into the personal computer operating system market (that they still dominate), leaving the long-term prospects for Windows® nowhere near as strong as they were pre-Windows Vista.

## Palm Inc's Cobalt Project

IN 1996 Palm Computing (then a division of U.S. Robotics) revolutionized handheld computing with the introduction of the wildly popular Palm Pilot.

Jeff Hawkins, Donna Dubinsky, and Ed Colligan founded Palm Computing with the original idea of creating Graffiti, a handwriting recognition software application, but later decided to create the first Palm Pilot 1000 and Pilot 5000 units as well. Between 1996 and 2003, PalmOne (as it became in 2003) experienced exceptional market penetration through improvements in both the Palm OS® by ACCESS operating system and hardware innovations (Palm OS® by ACCESS was not the name at that time; it was simply Palm OS).

By 2004 the picture had started to change. The reason was that Palm Computing had embarked on an IT project to deliver a Linux-based operating system named Cobalt that never saw the light of day.

Todd Kort, principal analyst in Gartner's Computing Platforms Worldwide group reported at the time that, "The decline in Palm OS market share in the first quarter of 2004 is not unexpected because many Palm OS users have delayed

PDA purchases until they can evaluate PalmSource's upcoming operating system Cobalt." PalmSource was the spin-off of a separate Palm OS software company from PalmOne.

Importantly, the popularity of Palm OS with its developer community was the key to PalmOne's success and the IT Project that was conceived to deliver Cobalt was intended to maintain both its market leadership position and the support of its developer community. PalmOne's hardware was revolutionary at the time, but what also drove their sales was the wealth of affordable software applications that ran on their handheld computers. This external value chain of software developers was vital to its success and had they profiled and disciplined their organization to not only heed, but support this value chain, their fortunes may not have waned as they have.

Palm Source's unilateral development strategy decision of June 2005 to halt all development efforts not related to Cobalt was intended to send a strong message to their developer community who, by that stage, were openly criticizing PalmOne and Palm Source for their inability to deliver on their promises. No devices with Cobalt emerged, and although the Treo™ Smartphone revitalized its market share, other than creating versions of Smart Phones for the Windows® Mobile operating system, they failed to deliver the promised Cobalt with a string of missed project deadlines, which estranged their developer community. Besides the direct costs of their failed IT project, the cost to the Palm brand has been to completely reverse their earlier position as market leader.

Palm's release of their Web O/S (a fully multitasking operating system) and the Palm Pre smart phone has been heralded by the pundits as a massive success but those same pundits acknowledge that Apple's iPhone and Google's Android phones have stolen too large a market share for Palm to regain its lost ground. Importantly, Apple created their "Apps" market where iPhone users have access to thousands of software applications written by independent software writers who are well supported by Apple. This is the same community that PalmSource, Access, and PalmOne estranged through their failed Cobalt project.

How Palm Inc. will fare from now on is anyone's guess but the developer communities are not taking any chances and are defecting in droves.

Had Palm Computing profiled its external value chain and fully understood and related to their developer community with timely and innovative releases of the Palm OS, the picture today may have been radically different.

# EPILOGUE

*"The men who try to do something and fail are infinitely better than those who try to do nothing and succeed"*

Lloyd Jones

# Epilogue

I  T project management principles that were established in the early 1970s have evolved to shape our accepted processes, management, and expected outcomes from IT implementations. Although these principles are fundamental to an IT project's success, this book has described how and why these processes need to be preceded by a rigorous pre-implementation corporate profiling process to reduce the incidence of IT project failures.

Even with proven project management methodologies in use, it's sad to see there is no end in sight to failed corporate IT projects and the extraordinary waste of time, money, and resources and the disastrous outcomes. The careers of good people fall by the wayside and the reputations of sound companies are tarnished, not to mention losses to shareholders. Lessons from past failures should give organizations reason enough to examine beforehand what they are contemplating doing and to be better prepared before investing in new IT projects. The examples cited in this book are a clear warning and a call for executives to ensure a rigorous analysis of requirements from all parties involved and to deliver a well—documented corporate profile before IT projects are initiated.

## Stop Blaming the Software

Although these concepts may be new to an organization, with this newfound understanding that the root causes of IT project failures are unlikely to be the software, vendors, the IT team, or project management methodologies, but rather a lack of corporate visibility, organizations must be prepared to undertake these corporate profiling initiatives. An organization's IT project pre-implementation processes need to be re-evaluated to ensure corporate profiling features prominently. Organizations may need to discard outdated notions that the all-important strategic IT decisions are made and executed in isolation, with little or no accountability from, or collaboration with, those who are best placed to speak on behalf of their groups. The alternative is to continue facing the risk of failure and the dire consequences.

The key issue at the heart of IT project failures is simply a lack of accountability by chief or senior executives for their IT investment and pre-implementation planning process decisions. This causes multiple failures everywhere in these projects because, beyond making the investment, there was no accountability for making high-level project process decisions, for establishing a pre-implementation process accurately identifying what the organization required, what the project needed, and what had to be done to ensure success. CIOs need to have a business orientation and completely understand how their organizations operate. More specifically, they need to understand what is different about their organization's needs to other businesses. Often project committees have people on board who know their part of the business, but there is no overriding "umbrella" view to give the necessary overall insight into how it all fits together and why it needs to fit the way it should. Consider the Airbus 380 that experienced major holdups because wiring looms did

# Epilogue

not fit correctly. It then becomes immediatcly clear that project failures are not the exclusive domain of IT, and that projects of any description can suffer from the same fate for the same common reasons when corporate profiling is not undertaken.

It's up to the organization whether it puts into practice the profiling concepts outlined in this book. But be warned that the success or failure of their next IT project rests entirely with an organization's senior executives and decision makers. If previous IT projects have failed yet projects continue to be initiated without profiling and an organization still expects a different result, they will be disappointed. I therefore urge all organizations to try a different approach and to profile their organizations ahead of their next pre-implementation process.

Please visit www.stopblamingthesoftware.com for tools, software and information that will assist you in creating and administering the corporate profiling process. Please feel free to email me directly with any queries at sjrunge@itpsb.com. I look forward to hearing from you.

# INDEX

# Index

# Index

# Index

# Index

# Index

# Index

## W

www.ingramcontent.com/pod-product-compliance
Lightning Source LLC
LaVergne TN
LVHW042138040326
832903LV00011B/291/J